2017 SQA Specimen and Past Papers with Answers

National 5
MODERN STUDIES

2015 & 2017 Exams
and 2017 Specimen Question Paper

HODDER
GIBSON
AN HACHETTE UK COMPANY

National 5 MODERN STUDIES

Hodder Gibson is grateful to the copyright holders, as credited on the final page of the Answer section, for permission to use their material. Every effort has been made to trace the copyright holders and to obtain their permission for the use of copyright material. Hodder Gibson will be happy to receive information allowing us to rectify any error or omission in future editions.

Hachette UK's policy is to use papers that are natural, renewable and recyclable products and made from wood grown in sustainable forests. The logging and manufacturing processes are expected to conform to the environmental regulations of the country of origin.

Orders: please contact Bookpoint Ltd, 130 Park Drive, Milton Park, Abingdon, Oxon OX14 4SE. Telephone: (44) 01235 827720. Fax: (44) 01235 400454. Lines are open 9.00–5.00, Monday to Saturday, with a 24-hour message answering service. Visit our website at www.hoddereducation.co.uk. Hodder Gibson can be contacted direct on: Tel: 0141 333 4650; Fax: 0141 404 8188; email: hoddergibson@hodder.co.uk

This collection first published in 2017 by
Hodder Gibson, an imprint of Hodder Education,
An Hachette UK Company
211 St Vincent Street
Glasgow G2 5QY

Typeset by Aptara, Inc.

Printed in the UK

A catalogue record for this title is available from the British Library

ISBN: 978-1-5104-2196-7

2 1

2018 2017

Introduction

National 5 Modern Studies

This book of SQA past papers contains the question papers used in the 2015* and 2017 exams (with the answers at the back of the book). The National 5 Modern Studies exam is being extended by 20 marks from 2018 onwards, following the removal of unit assessments from the course. A new specimen question paper, which reflects the requirements of the extended exam, is also included. The specimen question paper reflects the content and duration of the exam in 2018. All of the question papers included in the book (2015, 2017 and the new specimen question paper) provide excellent practice for the final exams.

Using the 2015 and 2017 past papers as part of your revision will help you to develop the vital skills and techniques needed for the exam, and will help you to identify any knowledge gaps you may have.

*Questions from the 2016 past paper have been used to create the new specimen question paper. To avoid duplication and provide you with optimum variety of questions, we have intentionally included the 2015 past paper instead.

The course

You will have studied the following three units:

- Democracy in Scotland and the United Kingdom
- Social Issues in the United Kingdom
- International Issues

Your teacher will usually have chosen one topic from each of the three sections above and you will answer questions on these in your exam (see table below).

SECTION 1	CHOICE ONE	CHOICE TWO
Democracy in Scotland and UK	A Democracy in Scotland	**OR** B Democracy in the UK
SECTION 2	CHOICE ONE	CHOICE TWO
Social Issues in the UK	C Social Inequality	**OR** D Crime and the Law
SECTION 3	CHOICE ONE	CHOICE TWO
International Issues	E World Powers	**OR** F World Issues

The Added Value unit for National 5 is an externally marked assessment. This consists of two parts:

- National 5 question paper
  80 marks allocated
  80% of marks
- National 5 assignment
  20 marks allocated
  20% of marks

Total marks available = 100

The marks you achieve in the question paper and assignment are added together and an overall mark will indicate a pass or fail. From this, your course award will then be graded.

Question paper

You will have 2 hours and 20 minutes to complete the question paper, with a total of 80 marks allocated. There are 30 marks available for skills-based questions and 50 for knowledge and understanding, with between 26 and 28 marks in total for each of the three exam sections as outlined in the table above.

In the exam paper, more marks are awarded for knowledge and understanding than skills so it is crucial that you have a sound grasp of content.

Each section will have four questions. There will be three questions assessing knowledge and understanding, and one question will assess evaluating skills using sources.

The four questions will be as follows:

Either one or two **Describe** (worth either 4, 6 or 8 marks) For example:

> Describe, in detail, at least two ways in which the police try to reduce crime levels.

Either one or two **Explain** (worth either 4, 6 or 8 marks) For example:

> Explain, in detail, why many people in the UK have good health while others do not.

Source-based (worth either 8 or 10 marks) For example:

> Using Sources 1, 2 and 3, what conclusions can be drawn about…?

What types of source-based questions will I need to answer?

There are three types of source-based skills questions and you will have practised these as class work. These three source-based skills questions are as follows:

- Supporting and opposing a view using a limited range of sources of information.
- Making and justifying a decision using a limited range of sources of information.
- Drawing and supporting conclusions using a limited range of sources of information.

Remember, in your course exam the skills based questions can appear in any of the three units – so drawing and supporting conclusions could be a question in the International Issues section of the exam.

Remember, in your course exam the knowledge and skills questions for International Issues will not refer to a particular country or issue. You will be expected to base your describe and explain answers around your knowledge and understanding of the World Power or World Issue you have studied.

What makes a good Knowledge and Understanding answer?

- Answer the question as set and only provide information relevant to the question.

- As far as you can, use up-to-date examples to illustrate your understanding of the question.

- Answer in detail and write in paragraphs with development of the points you wish to discuss. Remember, one very developed describe answer can gain 3 marks and one very developed explain answer can gain 4 marks.

- Show awareness of the difference between **describe** and **explain** questions and be able to answer appropriately.

- Use the number of marks given to each question as a guide to how much to write. Writing a long answer for a four mark question may cause you difficulty in completing the paper.

What makes a bad Knowledge and Understanding answer?

- Don't just write a list of facts. You will receive a maximum of two marks.

- Don't change the question to what you know – this is called *turning a question* and you will receive no marks for detailed description or explanation if it is not relevant.

- Avoid giving answers that are dated and too historical. This is especially a danger in the International Issues section.

- Don't rush together different issues, factors and explanations without developing your answer.

What makes a good Skills answer?

- Make full use of all the sources by linking evidence from more than one source to provide detailed arguments.

- Interpret statistical sources to indicate their significance to a question and how they link to other evidence.

- Make sure you use only the sources provided when writing your answers.

What makes a bad Skills answer?

- Don't use only a single piece of evidence from a source to provide argument.

- Don't simply repeat the statistical or written evidence without indicating its significance.

- Avoid bringing in your own knowledge of the issue or your own personal opinion.

Specific Skills advice

- For a selective use of facts answer, you should state whether the evidence being used is showing selectivity or not, and whether the evidence is supporting or opposing the view.

- For a conclusion answer, you should use the headings to draw an overall conclusion, which may be given at the beginning or end of the explanation.

- For a decision/recommendation answer, you should justify your decision and explain why you have rejected the other option.

Main changes to course assessment structure: question paper

- The exam time has increased to 2 hours and 20 minutes.

- There is greater emphasis on knowledge and understanding, with three knowledge and understanding (KU) questions now being asked.

- All skills questions will now have 10 marks each

- For a skills conclusion question, the number has been increased from three to four

Main changes to course content

Content of Democracy in Scotland and the United Kingdom has been reduced

- Local Government will no longer be examined. This includes the work of councillors and the electoral system used to elect councillors – Single Transferable Vote (STV).

- Explain why it is important to use your right to vote will also no longer be examined.

New addition

- Representation of women and minority groups will now be examined.

- Greater emphasis is now to be given to the purpose, function and composition of Committees in the Scottish Parliament.

International Issues

- In the World Powers section, the range of countries has been reduced from the G20, including the European Union, to now only include one of the G7 countries (excluding the UK) or one of the following: Brazil, China, India, Russia or South Africa.

- In the World Powers section, a minimum of three social and/or economic issues should be studied.

At least one issue covered should be a social issue and one an economic issue.

- In the World Issues section, the issue covered must be based on one of the following global issues:
  - a significant regional or international conflict (war or terrorism)
  - a significant regional or international economic issue
  - a significant regional or international humanitarian issue
- regional organisations (e.g. the African Union, NATO).

So you are now ready to answer the exam questions.

Good luck!

Remember that the rewards for passing National 5 Modern Studies are well worth it! Your pass will help you get the future you want for yourself. In the exam, be confident in your own ability. If you're not sure how to answer a question, trust your instincts and just give it a go anyway. Keep calm and don't panic! GOOD LUCK!

Introduction

Study Skills – what you need to know to pass exams!

Pause for thought

Many students might skip quickly through a page like this. After all, we all know how to revise. Do you really though?

Think about this:

"IF YOU ALWAYS DO WHAT YOU ALWAYS DO, YOU WILL ALWAYS GET WHAT YOU HAVE ALWAYS GOT."

Do you like the grades you get? Do you want to do better? If you get full marks in your assessment, then that's great! Change nothing! This section is just to help you get that little bit better than you already are.

There are two main parts to the advice on offer here. The first part highlights fairly obvious things but which are also very important. The second part makes suggestions about revision that you might not have thought about but which WILL help you.

Part 1

DOH! It's so obvious but …

Start revising in good time

Don't leave it until the last minute – this will make you panic.

Make a revision timetable that sets out work time AND play time.

Sleep and eat!

Obvious really, and very helpful. Avoid arguments or stressful things too – even games that wind you up. You need to be fit, awake and focused!

Know your place!

Make sure you know exactly **WHEN and WHERE** your exams are.

Know your enemy!

Make sure you know what to expect in the exam.

How is the paper structured?

How much time is there for each question?

What types of question are involved?

Which topics seem to come up time and time again?

Which topics are your strongest and which are your weakest?

Are all topics compulsory or are there choices?

Learn by DOING!

There is no substitute for past papers and practice papers – they are simply essential! Tackling this collection of papers and answers is exactly the right thing to be doing as your exams approach.

Part 2

People learn in different ways. Some like low light, some bright. Some like early morning, some like evening / night. Some prefer warm, some prefer cold. But everyone uses their BRAIN and the brain works when it is active. Passive learning – sitting gazing at notes – is the most INEFFICIENT way to learn anything. Below you will find tips and ideas for making your revision more effective and maybe even more enjoyable. What follows gets your brain active, and active learning works!

Activity 1 – Stop and review

Step 1

When you have done no more than 5 minutes of revision reading STOP!

Step 2

Write a heading in your own words which sums up the topic you have been revising.

Step 3

Write a summary of what you have revised in no more than two sentences. Don't fool yourself by saying, "I know it, but I cannot put it into words". That just means you don't know it well enough. If you cannot write your summary, revise that section again, knowing that you must write a summary at the end of it. Many of you will have notebooks full of blue/black ink writing. Many of the pages will not be especially attractive or memorable so try to liven them up a bit with colour as you are reviewing and rewriting. **This is a great memory aid, and memory is the most important thing.**

Activity 2 – Use technology!

Why should everything be written down? Have you thought about "mental" maps, diagrams, cartoons and colour to help you learn? And rather than write down notes, why not record your revision material?

What about having a text message revision session with friends? Keep in touch with them to find out how and what they are revising and share ideas and questions.

Why not make a video diary where you tell the camera what you are doing, what you think you have learned and what you still have to do? No one has to see or hear it, but the process of having to organise your thoughts in a formal way to explain something is a very important learning practice.

Be sure to make use of electronic files. You could begin to summarise your class notes. Your typing might be slow, but it will get faster and the typed notes will be easier to read than the scribbles in your class notes. Try to add different fonts and colours to make your work stand out. You can easily Google relevant pictures, cartoons and diagrams which you can copy and paste to make your work more attractive and **MEMORABLE**.

Activity 3 – This is it. Do this and you will know lots!

Step 1

In this task you must be very honest with yourself! Find the SQA syllabus for your subject (www.sqa.org.uk). Look at how it is broken down into main topics called MANDATORY knowledge. That means stuff you MUST know.

Step 2

BEFORE you do ANY revision on this topic, write a list of everything that you already know about the subject. It might be quite a long list but you only need to write it once. It shows you all the information that is already in your long-term memory so you know what parts you do not need to revise!

Step 3

Pick a chapter or section from your book or revision notes. Choose a fairly large section or a whole chapter to get the most out of this activity.

With a buddy, use Skype, Facetime, Twitter or any other communication you have, to play the game "If this is the answer, what is the question?". For example, if you are revising Geography and the answer you provide is "meander", your buddy would have to make up a question like "What is the word that describes a feature of a river where it flows slowly and bends often from side to side?".

Make up 10 "answers" based on the content of the chapter or section you are using. Give this to your buddy to solve while you solve theirs.

Step 4

Construct a wordsearch of at least 10 × 10 squares. You can make it as big as you like but keep it realistic. Work together with a group of friends. Many apps allow you to make wordsearch puzzles online. The words and phrases can go in any direction and phrases can be split. Your puzzle must only contain facts linked to the topic you are revising. Your task is to find 10 bits of information to hide in your puzzle, but you must not repeat information that you used in Step 3. DO NOT show where the words are. Fill up empty squares with random letters. Remember to keep a note of where your answers are hidden but do not show your friends. When you have a complete puzzle, exchange it with a friend to solve each other's puzzle.

Step 5

Now make up 10 questions (not "answers" this time) based on the same chapter used in the previous two tasks. Again, you must find NEW information that you have not yet used. Now it's getting hard to find that new information! Again, give your questions to a friend to answer.

Step 6

As you have been doing the puzzles, your brain has been actively searching for new information. Now write a NEW LIST that contains only the new information you have discovered when doing the puzzles. Your new list is the one to look at repeatedly for short bursts over the next few days. Try to remember more and more of it without looking at it. After a few days, you should be able to add words from your second list to your first list as you increase the information in your long-term memory.

FINALLY! Be inspired...

Make a list of different revision ideas and beside each one write **THINGS I HAVE** tried, **THINGS I WILL** try and **THINGS I MIGHT** try. Don't be scared of trying something new.

And remember – "FAIL TO PREPARE AND PREPARE TO FAIL!"

NATIONAL 5
2015

National Qualifications 2015

X749/75/11

Modern Studies

WEDNESDAY, 27 MAY
9:00 AM – 10:45 AM

Total marks — 60

SECTION 1 — DEMOCRACY IN SCOTLAND AND THE UNITED KINGDOM — 20 marks

Attempt ONE part, EITHER

SECTION 2 — SOCIAL ISSUES IN THE UNITED KINGDOM — 20 marks

Attempt ONE part, EITHER

SECTION 3 — INTERNATIONAL ISSUES — 20 marks

Attempt ONE part, EITHER

Write your answers clearly in the answer booklet provided. In the answer booklet you must clearly identify the question number you are attempting.

Use **blue** or **black** ink.

Before leaving the examination room you must give your answer booklet to the Invigilator; if you do not, you may lose all the marks for this paper.

MARKS

SECTION 1 — DEMOCRACY IN SCOTLAND AND THE UNITED KINGDOM — 20 marks

Attempt ONE part, either

Part A — Democracy in Scotland   on pages 2–5

OR

Part B — Democracy in the United Kingdom   on pages 6–9

PART A — DEMOCRACY IN SCOTLAND

In your answers to Questions 1 and 2 you should give recent examples from Scotland.

Question 1

Local councils provide many services in Scotland.

Describe, **in detail**, **two** services provided by local councils in Scotland.   4

Question 2

People in Scotland can participate in society in many ways.

Explain, **in detail**, why some people participate in **one** of the following:

- Pressure Groups
- Trade Unions
- The Media.   6

[Turn over for Question 3 on *Page four*]

DO NOT WRITE ON THIS PAGE

PART A (continued)

Question 3

Study Sources 1, 2 and 3 and then answer the question which follows.

Glenlochy is about to elect a new MSP. You are a voter in Glenlochy. You are undecided between Option 1 and Option 2.

Using sources 1, 2 and 3 you must decide which option to choose.

Option 1 Daisy Frost, candidate for the Scottish Labour Party	**Option 2** Tom Kirk, candidate for the Scottish National Party

SOURCE 1

Daisy Frost

Age 56

Studied Politics at Abertay University

Currently a local councillor

If I am elected to represent Glenlochy I will work to ensure that more women are elected to the Scottish Parliament. I believe that the lack of women in Holyrood has affected the number of women working locally. This needs to change.

Unemployment is clearly a problem in the local area and I would work hard to increase job opportunities. A lack of internet access is an obvious barrier and I would seek to improve this.

Crime is not a major concern so I would not focus on this if elected but would try to increase access to childcare as this is important to the community. Health care is an area I am passionate about and health in Glenlochy needs to improve. The lives of the people of Glenlochy are being cruelly cut short and I pledge to change this.

Tom Kirk

Age 35

Studied Law at Aberdeen University

Currently a lawyer for Citizens' Advice

Employment is a key area which I will try to improve if elected. Too few local people are in full-time work. This means that too many are also relying on benefits to get by.

I will work hard to ensure that the elderly of Glenlochy continue to be treated with dignity and feel safe in the local community. The majority of local people agree with me that elderly people are well cared for.

Skills education is key to any improvements in Glenlochy. Unfortunately at the moment too many local children are leaving school before S6 without the skills they need.

Childcare is not a major concern so I would not focus on this if elected but would try to decrease crime as this is a major concern in the community.

PART A Question 3 (continued)   MARKS

SOURCE 2

Selected Facts about Glenlochy

Glenlochy is a constituency for the Scottish Parliament in central Scotland. This part of Scotland used to rely on coal mining as its main industry. There is now only one major employer, a call centre in the main town of Glenlochy. Last month it made 100 full-time workers redundant. Parts of the area are amongst the most deprived in Scotland and there are few job opportunities. Average life expectancy in the area is 77 compared to a Scottish average of 79.

Glenlochy Constituency is holding a by-election due to the death of the previous MSP. Many people feel the area now needs an experienced representative.

There was a local meeting about crime levels last month in the town hall where 530 residents turned up to speak to the local community police officer about their concerns. Carol Fife, Chair of the Community Council said "Crime is clearly increasing. We are very worried about this issue. Our new MSP needs to have a legal background".

Opinion Poll of 1000 Glenlochy Residents

	The elderly are well looked after in Glenlochy	Crime is a problem in Glenlochy	The Scottish Parliament needs more female MSPs	A lack of childcare is a major problem locally
Strongly agree	12%	30%	21%	36%
Agree	23%	35%	33%	32%
Disagree	25%	26%	25%	22%
Strongly disagree	40%	9%	21%	10%

SOURCE 3

Glenlochy Statistics (%)

	Glenlochy	Scotland
Unemployed and seeking work	9	7
Claiming benefits	17·5	15·8
Full-time employment	42	48
Women in work	34	45
Suffering long-term ill health	15	18
Pupils completing S6 at school	56	54
Households with internet access	79	76

You must decide which option to recommend, **either** Daisy Frost (**Option 1**) **or** Tom Kirk (**Option 2**).

(i)   Using Sources 1, 2 and 3, **which option would you choose?**

(ii)   Give reasons to **support** your choice.

(iii)   **Explain** why you did not choose the other option.

Your answer **must** be based on all three sources.   10

NOW GO TO SECTION 2 ON *PAGE TEN*

MARKS

PART B — DEMOCRACY IN THE UNITED KINGDOM

In your answers to Questions 4 and 5 you should give recent examples from the United Kingdom.

Question 4

> The House of Lords has an important role in the UK Government.

Describe, **in detail**, **two** of the roles the House of Lords has in the UK Government.

4

Question 5

> People in the UK can participate in society in many ways.

Explain, **in detail**, why some people participate in **one** of the following:

- Pressure Groups
- Trade Unions
- The Media.

6

[Turn over for Question 6 on *Page eight*]

DO NOT WRITE ON THIS PAGE

PART B (continued)

Question 6

Study Sources 1, 2 and 3 and then answer the question which follows.

Millwood is about to elect a new MP. You are a voter in Millwood. You are undecided between Option 1 and Option 2

Using sources 1, 2 and 3 you must decide which option to choose.

| **Option 1** Nora Manson, candidate for the Scottish Conservative Party | **Option 2** John Donaldson, candidate for the Scottish Liberal Democratic Party |

SOURCE 1

BestPals   🏠 Home   ⚙ Settings   ▼ | Search | 🔍

Nora Manson
Age 56
Studied Politics at Glasgow University
Currently a local councillor
Born in Millwood

John Donaldson
Age 35
Studied Law at Edinburgh University
Currently a lawyer for Citizens' Advice
Born in Millwood

If I am elected to represent Millwood I will work to ensure that more women are elected to the UK parliament. I believe that the lack of women in Westminster has an effect on the number of women working locally. This needs to change.

Unemployment is clearly a problem in the local area and I would work hard to increase job opportunities. A lack of internet access is an obvious barrier and I would seek to improve this.

Crime is not a major concern so I would not focus on this if elected but would try to increase access to childcare as this is important to the community. Health care is an area I am passionate about and health in Millwood needs to improve. The lives of the people of Millwood are being cruelly cut short and I pledge to change this.

Employment is a key area which I will try to improve if elected. Too few local people are in full-time work. This means that too many are also relying on benefits to get by.

I will work hard to ensure that the elderly of Millwood are treated with dignity and feel safe in the local community. The majority of local people agree with me that elderly people are well cared for.

Skills education is vital if improvements are to be made. At the moment too many local children are leaving school before S6 without the skills they need.

Childcare is not a major concern so I would not focus on this if elected, but would try to decrease crime as this is a major concern in the community.

PART B Question 6 (continued)   MARKS

SOURCE 2

Selected Facts about Millwood

Millwood is a constituency for the UK Parliament in central Scotland. This part of Scotland used to rely on steelmaking as its main industry. There is now only one major employer, a call centre in the main town of Millwood. Last month it made 100 full-time workers redundant. Parts of the area are amongst the most deprived in the UK and there are few job opportunities. Average life expectancy in the area is 77 compared to a UK average of 80.

Millwood Constituency is holding a by-election due to the death of the previous MP. Many people feel the area now needs an experienced representative.

There was a local meeting about crime levels last month in the town hall where 530 residents turned up to speak to the local community police officer about their concerns. Lynn Morrow, Chair of the Community Council said "Crime is clearly increasing. We are very worried about this issue. Our new MP needs to have a legal background".

Opinion Poll of 1000 Millwood Residents

	The elderly are well looked after in Millwood	Crime is a problem in Millwood	The UK Parliament needs more female MPs	A lack of childcare is a major problem locally
Strongly agree	12%	26%	21%	36%
Agree	23%	35%	33%	32%
Disagree	25%	30%	25%	22%
Strongly disagree	40%	9%	21%	10%

SOURCE 3

Millwood Statistics (%)

	Millwood	UK
Unemployed and seeking work	9	6
Claiming benefits	17·5	15·2
Full-time employment	42	49
Women in work	34	45
Suffering long-term ill health	15	18
Pupils completing S6 at school	56	53
Households with internet access	79	77

You must decide which option to recommend, **either** Nora Manson (**Option 1**) **or** John Donaldson (**Option 2**).

(i)   Using Sources 1, 2 and 3, **which option would you choose**?

(ii)   Give reasons to **support** your choice.

(iii)   **Explain** why you did not choose the other option.

Your answer **must** be based on all three sources.   10

NOW GO TO SECTION 2 ON *PAGE TEN*

MARKS

SECTION 2 — SOCIAL ISSUES IN THE UNITED KINGDOM — 20 marks

Attempt ONE part, either

Part C — Social Inequality   on pages 10–13

OR

Part D — Crime and the Law   on pages 14–17

PART C — SOCIAL INEQUALITY

In your answers to Questions 7 and 8 you should give recent examples from the United Kingdom.

Question 7

The UK Government tries to reduce social inequality.

Describe, **in detail**, **two** ways in which the UK Government tries to reduce social inequality.

4

Question 8

There are many groups in the UK which experience inequality.

Explain, **in detail**, the reasons why one or more groups you have studied experiences inequality in the UK.

8

[Turn over for Question 9 on *Page twelve*]

DO NOT WRITE ON THIS PAGE

PART C (continued)

Question 9

Study Sources 1, 2 and 3 and then answer the question which follows.

SOURCE 1

Poverty Factfile (2013 – 2014)

There are still 3·6 million children living in poverty in the United Kingdom. This means that a quarter (25%) of children in the UK currently live in poverty.

According to the UK Government, an average family needs to have £349 each week to meet their basic needs. The reality of living in poverty means that many families have only about £12 per day, per person to cover the basic cost of living. Children living in poverty often go without the items many children take for granted such as a bike or going on a school trip.

Poverty also has a negative impact on the health of a child with poor children experiencing more ill health than richer children. In addition, 24% of the poorest families cannot afford to keep their house warm compared to just 3% of wealthy families.

The UK Government is trying to reduce the problem of poverty. It recently set the ambitious targets that no more than 4% of children will be living in absolute poverty with a target of 12% for relative poverty by the year 2020. Absolute poverty is when someone cannot afford the basic necessities of life eg food, shelter. Relative poverty is in comparison to average incomes within a country.

Living in poverty can reduce a child's expectation of their own life and can often lead to a lifetime of poverty. Many people believe that it is the government's responsibility to help children improve their life chances and escape the cycle of poverty.

SOURCE 2

Selected Family Statistics

	Children Living in the Poorest Families	Children Living in the Richest Families
Average life expectancy at birth (years)	71	82
Childhood obesity rates	25%	18%
Average weekly family spending on food	£49	£70
Families who cannot afford a week's holiday per year	62%	6%

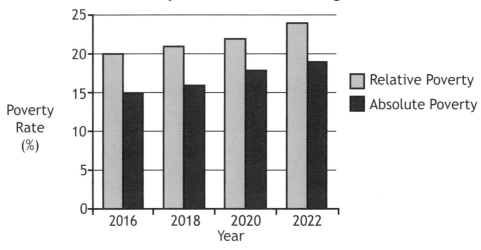

Estimated Child Poverty Rates in the United Kingdom 2016 – 2022

MARKS

PART C Question 9 (continued)

SOURCE 3

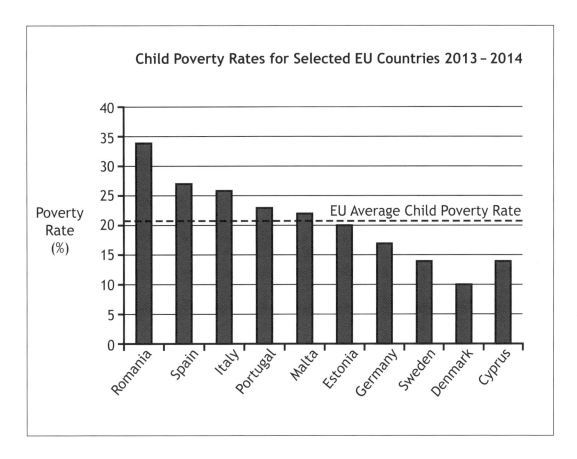

Child Poverty Rates for Selected EU Countries 2013 – 2014

Using Sources 1, 2 and 3, what **conclusions** can be drawn about the issue of child poverty.

You should reach a conclusion about **each** of the following.

- The impact of poverty on a child's life
- The UK Government's progress towards meeting its targets for 2020
- UK child poverty rates compared to other countries

Your conclusions **must** be supported by evidence from the sources. You should link information within and between the sources in support of your conclusions.

Your answer **must** be based on all three sources.   **8**

NOW GO TO SECTION 3 ON *PAGE EIGHTEEN*

MARKS

PART D — CRIME AND THE LAW

In your answers to Questions 10 and 11 you should give recent examples from the United Kingdom.

Question 10

Scottish courts have the power to punish people.

Describe, **in detail**, **two** different ways that Scottish Courts can punish people.   4

Question 11

There are many factors which cause crime in the UK.

Explain, **in detail**, the factors which cause crime in the UK.   8

[Turn over for Question 12 on *Page sixteen*]

DO NOT WRITE ON THIS PAGE

PART D (continued)

Question 12

Study Sources 1, 2 and 3 below and then answer the question which follows.

SOURCE 1

Social Media and the Law

The law that has been used to prosecute people for sending inappropriate messages via social media is section 127 of the Communications Act 2003.

This states that a person is guilty of an offence if they send, post or forward a message online that is offensive or of an indecent, obscene or menacing character.

Social Media has become an important part of all areas of our daily lives. However, only one in five people (19%) read the terms and conditions of sites, and only one in ten know about social media laws, or have heard of the Communications Act 2003.

Communications sent via social media can be classed as criminal offences and companies now have more rules about the use of social media in their contracts and policies. A growing number of employers are now using social media sites to investigate people who have applied for a job. When surveyed, 63% of 16 to 18 year olds wrongly believed that this was against the law.

It is an offence to cause distress or threaten individuals online and those who embark on "trolling" can expect to be prosecuted by the police. Many people feel that they can behave differently online as they believe they are anonymous. However, more and more people are being prosecuted for their online activities and have received punishments from the courts.

Some police forces recognise that this is a very serious problem but they are extremely concerned that resources are being wasted — they estimate that two thirds of incidents reported to them are for petty online arguments.

SOURCE 2

Memo to Employees

GLENINCH COUNCIL

Dear Employees,

A recent University report suggests that the Scottish economy is
losing millions of pounds because of workers using social media inappropriately during work time. Social media breaks are now costing us more than cigarette breaks!

Many of you will already be using social media in a variety of ways in your lives outside work. This memo will help you use social media responsibly at work.

We recognise the opportunities offered by social media and would like staff to use it to enhance the work of the Council.

However, you must respect the needs of the Council to protect its reputation.

If you use social media irresponsibly there is a risk that the Council will be damaged. We expect you to use social media responsibly and with care. If you do not do this you could be disciplined, face the sack or be prosecuted by the police. Sending inappropriate messages or taking social media breaks when you are supposed to be working will not be tolerated.

PART D Question 12 (continued)

SOURCE 3

Social Media Statistics

Opinion Poll
Question — Are you aware of the possible consequences of sending an offensive Tweet?

Yes	25%
No	75%

Social media – Complaints and prosecutions

	Complaints made to police about offensive posts on social media	Successful prosecutions
2010	2,347	60
2011	2,490	90
2012	2,563	107
2013	2,672	142
2014	2,703	240

Hours lost through social media breaks throughout the UK

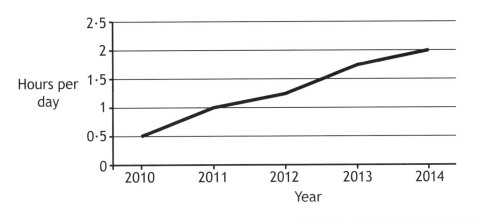

Using Sources 1, 2 and 3, what **conclusions** can be drawn about the law concerning social media.

You should reach a conclusion about each of the following:

- The level of public awareness of the law concerning social media
- Social media and the workplace
- Crime associated with social media.

Your conclusions must be supported by evidence from the sources. You should link information within and between the sources in support of your conclusions.

Your answer must be based on all three sources.

8

NOW GO TO SECTION 3 ON *PAGE EIGHTEEN*

MARKS

SECTION 3 — INTERNATIONAL ISSUES — 20 marks

Attempt ONE part, either

Part E — World Powers   on pages 18–21

OR

Part F — World Issues   on pages 22–25

PART E — WORLD POWERS

In your answers to Questions 13 and 14 you should give recent examples from a world power you have studied.

Question 13

> World Powers can have an impact on other countries.

Describe, **in detail**, **two ways** the World Power you have studied has had an impact on other countries.

In your answer you should state the world power you have studied.   6

Question 14

> In all World Powers, some groups of people are poorly represented in government.

Explain, **in detail**, why some groups of people are poorly represented in the government of the world power you have studied.

In your answer you should state the world power you have studied.   6

[Turn over for Question 15 on *Page twenty*]

DO NOT WRITE ON THIS PAGE

PART E (continued)

Question 15

Study Sources 1, 2 and 3 and then answer the question which follows.

Source 1

Gun Ownership in Selected G20 Countries

 USA — Guns : *ALLOWED*

According to the US Constitution all Americans can own a gun. A US Government report found that gun ownership increased from 192 million firearms in 1994 to 310 million firearms in 2009, but levels of crime fell sharply. Gun control campaigners argue that the easy availability of guns increases crime. The Brady Campaign to Prevent Gun Violence found that the US firearm homicide rate is 20 times higher than the combined rates of 22 countries with similar levels of wealth. A study from Harvard University said "there is no evidence which proves widespread gun ownership among the general population leads to higher incidents of murder."

FRANCE — Guns: *ALLOWED*  **JAPAN — Guns: *BANNED***

Rules around gun ownership are strict eg you must see a doctor every year to get a certificate to prove you are physically and mentally able.

The weapons law begins by stating "No-one shall possess a firearm or firearms or a sword or swords", and very few exceptions are allowed.

BRAZIL — Guns: *ALLOWED* **INDIA — Guns: *BANNED***

In 2004, the number of gun-related injuries was 36,000. Despite this, in a 2005 referendum, 65% of the Brazilian population voted against banning the sale of guns and ammunition.

The law prevents the sale, manufacture, possession, import, export and transport of firearms and ammunition.

 RUSSIA — Guns: *BANNED*

Ownership of most types of guns is illegal for Russian civilians. Despite this, public shootings still happen. In November 2012, 30-year-old lawyer Dmitry Vinogradov walked into the Moscow offices of a medical company where he worked, and opened fire on his colleagues — murdering six and critically injuring one more. Right to Bear Arms, a Moscow based pressure group which represents gun owners, claimed "We have conducted studies which identify a clear pattern: the more a society is armed, the lower the level of criminal violence."

PART E Question 15 (continued)

Source 2

More Guns = More Deaths?

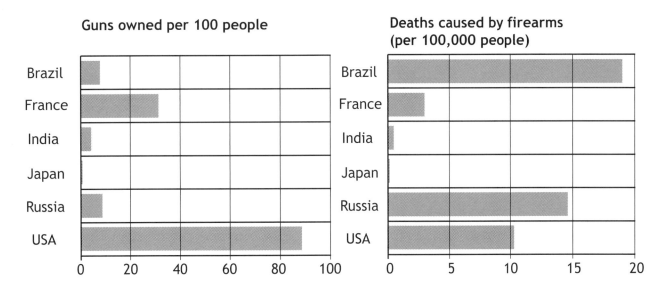

Guns owned per 100 people

Deaths caused by firearms
(per 100,000 people)

SOURCE 3

Crime Statistics

Country	Murder Rate per 100,000	Violent Crime per 100,000	Robbery per 100,000
Brazil	27	504	110
France	1·65	201	100·8
India	1·5	162	1·6
Japan	0·4	98	4·0
Russia	10·2	584	90·3
USA	4·7	386	146·4

Using Sources 1, 2 and 3, explain why the view of **Kristen Nunez is selective in the use of facts**.

> Countries which allow gun ownership are safer places to live.
>
> View of Kristen Nunez

In your answer you must:

- give evidence from the sources that supports Kristen Nunez's view

and

- give evidence from the sources that opposes Kristen Nunez's view.

Your answer **must** be based on all three sources.

8

MARKS

PART F — WORLD ISSUES

In your answers to Questions 16 and 17 you should give recent examples from a world issue you have studied.

Question 16

Ordinary people are often affected by international issues and conflicts.

Describe, **in detail**, **two** ways ordinary people have been affected by an international issue **or** conflict you have studied.

In your answer you should state the world issue or conflict you have studied.

6

Question 17

International Organisations attempt to resolve issues and conflicts.

Selected International Organisations		
United Nations	NATO	European Union
Charities	NGOs	African Union

Select an International Organisation you have studied.

Explain, in detail, the reasons why it has succeeded **or** failed in resolving an international issue **or** conflict.

In your answer you should state the world issue or conflict you have studied.

6

[Turn over for Question 18 on *Page twenty-four*]

DO NOT WRITE ON THIS PAGE

PART F (continued)

Question 18

Study Sources 1, 2 and 3 and then answer the question which follows.

Source 1

Illegal Drug Producers and Users

Drug producer: Afghanistan - Heroin and Marijuana

Afghanistan produces more opium than any other country in the world. Crops have dropped by 10% recently and the President recently stated that "Afghanistan is now a safer place to live." Almost all of the heroin used in Europe comes from Afghanistan's opium fields. In addition Afghanistan also supplies large amounts of marijuana to the world. Two aid workers travelling in Herat city were shot dead by an armed drug gang in July 2014.

Drug Producer: Peru - Cocaine and Heroin

Peru is the second largest producer of cocaine in the world. Until 1996, Peru was number one, but was then overtaken by Colombia.

Drug producer: Colombia - Cocaine

Colombia produces more cocaine than any other country in the world. They provide almost all of the cocaine consumed in the United States, as well as in other countries. Certain parts of the country are "no-go" areas for tourists and the police.

Drug user: The USA – Marijuana

Over 51% of all American adults have used marijuana at some stage in their lives. This is the highest figure in the world. Criminal gangs make billions of dollars and recently one gang member admitted to murdering forty enemies from other gangs. In a recent speech, President Obama stressed that the murder rate in the USA had halved in the last twenty years.

Drug user: Iran – Heroin

Iran has one of the highest rates of heroin use in the world. 2·3% of adults have used heroin in the last year.

Drug user: El Salvador - Cocaine

The small Central American country of El Salvador has a big issue with cocaine use. One in every forty people are regular users. Around 60 000 people are members of organised criminal gangs but the government has reduced the murder rate by 80% in recent years.

PART F Question 18 (continued)

Source 2

More Drugs = More Crime?

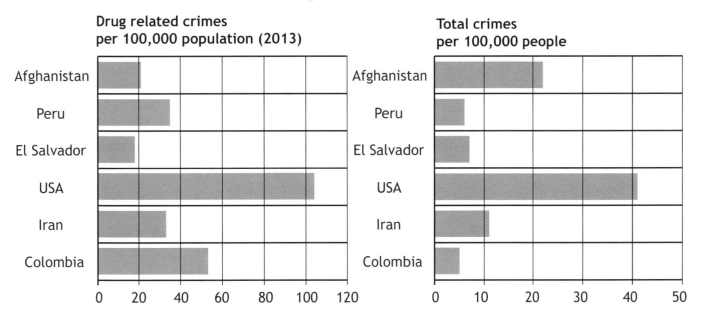

Drug related crimes per 100,000 population (2013)

Total crimes per 100,000 people

SOURCE 3

Crime Statistics

Country	Murder Rate per 100,000	Violent Kidnappings per 100,000	Serious Assaults per 100,000
Afghanistan	3·4	56	33
Peru	5·7	46	100
El Salvador	57·5	0·1	176
USA	4·7	17	874
Iran	3·9	4	44
Colombia	61·1	65	63

Using Sources 1, 2 and 3, explain why the view of **Ted King is selective in the use of facts.**

> Countries which produce illegal drugs are more dangerous places to live.
>
> View of Ted King

In your answer you must:

- give evidence from the sources that supports Ted King's view

and

- give evidence from the sources that opposes Ted King's view.

Your answer **must** be based on all three sources.

8

[END OF QUESTION PAPER]

[BLANK PAGE]

DO NOT WRITE ON THIS PAGE

NATIONAL 5

2017

FRIDAY, 19 MAY

1:00 PM – 2:45 PM

Total marks — 60

SECTION 1 — DEMOCRACY IN SCOTLAND AND THE UNITED KINGDOM — 20 marks

Attempt ONE part, EITHER

SECTION 2 — SOCIAL ISSUES IN THE UNITED KINGDOM — 20 marks

Attempt ONE part, EITHER

SECTION 3 — INTERNATIONAL ISSUES — 20 marks

Attempt ONE part, EITHER

Write your answers clearly in the answer booklet provided. In the answer booklet you must clearly identify the question number you are attempting.

Use **blue** or **black** ink.

Before leaving the examination room you must give your answer booklet to the Invigilator; if you do not, you may lose all the marks for this paper.

MARKS

SECTION 1 — DEMOCRACY IN SCOTLAND AND THE UNITED KINGDOM — 20 marks

Attempt ONE part, either

Part A — Democracy in Scotland   on pages 02—05

OR

Part B — Democracy in the United Kingdom   on pages 06—09

PART A — DEMOCRACY IN SCOTLAND

In your answers to Questions 1 and 2 you should give recent examples from Scotland.

Question 1

People in Scotland have many political rights.

Describe, **in detail, two** political rights that people in Scotland have.   4

Question 2

Some political parties' election campaigns are successful during Scottish Parliament elections.

Explain, **in detail**, the reasons why some political parties' election campaigns are successful during Scottish Parliament elections.

You should give a **maximum of three reasons** in your answer.   8

[Turn over for next question

DO NOT WRITE ON THIS PAGE

PART A (continued)

Question 3

Study Sources 1, 2 and 3 and then answer the question which follows.

SOURCE 1

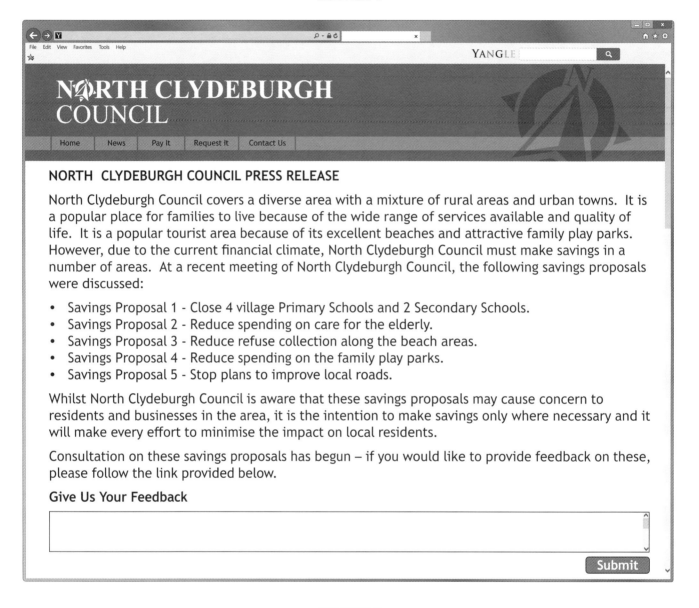

NORTH CLYDEBURGH COUNCIL PRESS RELEASE

North Clydeburgh Council covers a diverse area with a mixture of rural areas and urban towns. It is a popular place for families to live because of the wide range of services available and quality of life. It is a popular tourist area because of its excellent beaches and attractive family play parks. However, due to the current financial climate, North Clydeburgh Council must make savings in a number of areas. At a recent meeting of North Clydeburgh Council, the following savings proposals were discussed:

- Savings Proposal 1 - Close 4 village Primary Schools and 2 Secondary Schools.
- Savings Proposal 2 - Reduce spending on care for the elderly.
- Savings Proposal 3 - Reduce refuse collection along the beach areas.
- Savings Proposal 4 - Reduce spending on the family play parks.
- Savings Proposal 5 - Stop plans to improve local roads.

Whilst North Clydeburgh Council is aware that these savings proposals may cause concern to residents and businesses in the area, it is the intention to make savings only where necessary and it will make every effort to minimise the impact on local residents.

Consultation on these savings proposals has begun – if you would like to provide feedback on these, please follow the link provided below.

Give Us Your Feedback

SOURCE 2

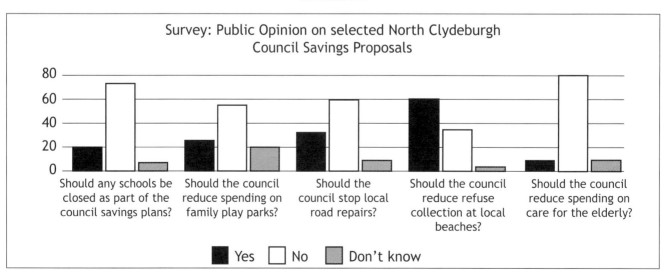

Survey: Public Opinion on selected North Clydeburgh Council Savings Proposals

SOURCE 2 (continued) MARKS

NORTH CLYDEBURGH COUNCIL: SAVINGS FROM EACH PROPOSAL (total=£70 million)

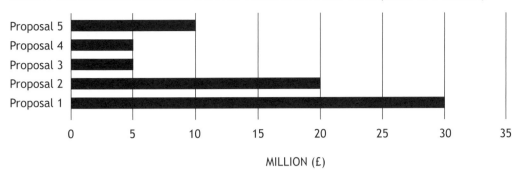

MILLION (£)

SOURCE 3

CLYDEBURGH HERALD

COUNCIL MUST MAKE HARD CHOICES TO SAVE CASH

Local Councillors must agree on a plan to save money from their budget. The council has a savings target of £75 million.

North Clydeburgh is a local authority with a population of approximately 150,000. Schools in the area are considered to be excellent and education has always been a high priority for the council.

It also has many important leisure and tourist attractions including award winning beaches. The tourist industry is an important employer in the area. If the standard of the beaches were to fall tourists may choose to go elsewhere. This would lead to many job losses.

A significant number of North Clydeburgh's population are elderly and rely on the services provided by the council. Recently the leader of North Clydeburgh Council said, "elderly care is a very important part of the services the council provides. It is essential that North Clydeburgh Council spends an extra £10 million this year on meeting the growing demands of care for the elderly. We must find this extra money to improve council services for our elderly population."

A local pressure group has said that at least £5 million must be spent on improving the transport system in North Clydeburgh. The pressure group believes this money must be spent on repairing pot holes and poor road surfaces.

Clearly North Clydeburgh Council has some very tough decisions to make in the next few weeks.

Using Sources 1, 2 and 3, what **conclusions** can be drawn about North Clydeburgh Council's savings proposals?

You should reach a conclusion about each of the following:

- The public support in North Clydeburgh for Savings Proposal 3.
- The impact of Savings Proposal 2 on council services.
- The success of North Clydeburgh Council in achieving its savings target.

Your conclusions must be supported by evidence from the sources. You should link information within and between the sources in support of your conclusions.

Your answer **must** be based on all **three** sources. 8

NOW GO TO SECTION 2 ON PAGE 10

MARKS

PART B — DEMOCRACY IN THE UNITED KINGDOM

In your answers to Questions 4 and 5 you should give recent examples from the United Kingdom.

Question 4

> People in the UK have many political rights.

Describe, **in detail, two** political rights that people in the UK have.

4

Question 5

> Some political parties' election campaigns are successful during General Elections.

Explain, **in detail**, the reasons why some political parties' election campaigns are successful during General Elections.

You should give a **maximum of three reasons** in your answer.

8

[Turn over for next question

DO NOT WRITE ON THIS PAGE

PART B (continued)

Question 6

Study Sources 1, 2 and 3 and then answer the question which follows.

SOURCE 1

2015 General Election Results Analysis

At 10pm on election night, based on exit polls, political analysts correctly predicted that the Conservatives were way out in front and would in fact be the single biggest party in the House of Commons. So unexpected were the exit poll results that some commentators claimed that they could not possibly be correct.

The performance of some smaller political parties also demonstrated that the UK electoral map is changing. The Green Party, while only managing to secure one MP to the Commons, significantly increased their percentage share of the vote from the 2010 election. The popularity of UKIP was also evident with the party securing over 3·8 million votes, returning one MP to the House of Commons. On the other hand the Liberal Democrats did not fare as well with a significant drop in both their UK share of the vote and the number of MPs returned to the House of Commons.

In Scotland the political landscape changed. The "Red-Lands" of Labour were crushed by the Scottish National Party under the leadership of Nicola Sturgeon. The Scotsman newspaper ran with the headline that the SNP result would be "A night that will change Britain forever". The election of 56 SNP Members of Parliament also saw the election of the youngest MP to the House of Commons. Mhairi Black won the constituency of Paisley and Renfrewshire South with a comfortable majority.

SOURCE 2

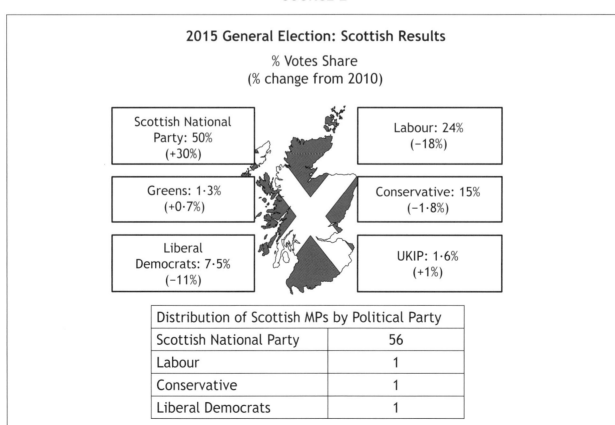

2015 General Election: Scottish Results

% Votes Share
(% change from 2010)

Scottish National Party: 50%
(+30%)

Labour: 24%
(−18%)

Greens: 1·3%
(+0·7%)

Conservative: 15%
(−1·8%)

Liberal Democrats: 7·5%
(−11%)

UKIP: 1·6%
(+1%)

Distribution of Scottish MPs by Political Party	
Scottish National Party	56
Labour	1
Conservative	1
Liberal Democrats	1

MARKS

PART B Question 6 (continued)

SOURCE 3

2015 General Election Results by Seats			
Party	No of Seats	% of Seats	Change since 2010
Conservative	331	51%	+24 Seats
Labour	232	35%	−26 Seats
UKIP	1	<1%	No Change
SNP	56	9%	+50 Seats
Liberal Democrats	8	2%	−49 Seats
Greens	1	<1%	No change

% Share of the UK Vote for Selected General Elections

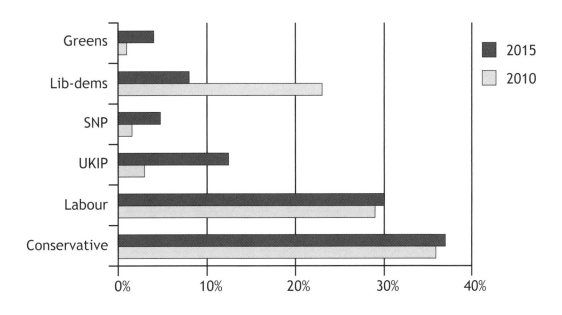

Using Sources 1, 2 and 3, what **conclusions** can be drawn about the 2015 General Election?

You should reach a conclusion about each of the following:

- The UK electoral performance of the Conservative Party compared to 2010.
- The UK electoral performance of the Liberal Democrats compared to 2010.
- The dominant political party in Scotland after the General Election.

Your conclusions must be supported by evidence from the sources. You should link information within and between the sources in support of your conclusions.

Your answer **must** be based on all **three** sources.

8

NOW GO TO SECTION 2 ON PAGE 10

MARKS

SECTION 2 — SOCIAL ISSUES IN THE UNITED KINGDOM — 20 marks

Attempt ONE part, either

Part C — Social Inequality   on pages 10–13

OR

Part D — Crime and the Law   on pages 14–17

PART C — SOCIAL INEQUALITY

In your answers to Questions 7 and 8 you should give recent examples from the United Kingdom.

Question 7

> There are many consequences of social inequalities on communities.

Describe, **in detail, two** consequences of social inequalities on communities.   **6**

Question 8

> Some people are more likely to suffer social inequalities than others.

Explain, **in detail, two** reasons why some people are more likely to suffer social inequalities than others.   **6**

[Turn over for next question

DO NOT WRITE ON THIS PAGE

PART C (continued)

Question 9

Study Sources 1, 2 and 3 and then answer the question which follows.

SOURCE 1

| Home | How it works | Get involved | News and Events | Contact us |

UK Foodbanks

Our foodbank is part of a UK-wide foodbank network run by Emergency Assistance Trust (EAT).The Trust was launched in 2005 and we provide help for those in severe need. The Trust partners with community organisations to open new foodbanks across the UK. Each foodbank is run as an independent charity but the EAT provides training and support. With over 400 foodbanks currently launched, and three new ones opening every week, the EAT's goal is for every town to have one.

Why do people need emergency food?

There has been a doubling of food poverty over the last four years and now it is estimated that 4.7 million Brits are living in food poverty. Wages haven't kept up with the rising cost of food - it is predicted that the average household food bill will rise by £357 by 2017. Today people across the UK will struggle to feed themselves and their families for a number of different reasons and foodbanks help to prevent crime, housing loss, family breakdown and mental health problems. A simple box of food makes a big difference. ***Read client stories***

What do foodbanks do?

- Last year the EAT foodbank network fed over 1 million people who would have been hungry without this essential service.
- All food is donated by the public and sorted by volunteers.
- To get a foodbox, applicants must first be referred by a recognised agency, for example their GP or social worker, who issue food vouchers.
- Clients receive three days of nutritionally balanced, non perishable food in exchange for their food voucher. Foodbanks also make time to chat and direct clients to other helpful services such as debt advice and career guidance.

> Each foodbox contains a minimum of three days' nutritionally balanced non-perishable food. Foodbanks rely on the support of local communities. **Click here** to help your nearest foodbank in your area.
>
> If there's no foodbank near you why not find out more about **starting a foodbank.**

What's in a foodbox?

Milk (UHT or powdered)
Sugar (500g)
Fruit juice (carton)
Soup
Pasta sauces
Sponge pudding (tinned)
Tomatoes (tinned)
Cereals
Rice pudding (tinned)
Tea bags/instant coffee
Instant mash potato
Rice/pasta
Tinned meat/fish
Tinned vegetables
Tinned fruit
Jam
Biscuits or snack bar

DONATE

How many people use Foodbanks?

2012-2013	2013-2014	2014-2015	2015-2016
346,992	913,138	1,084,604	1,109,309

PART C Question 9 (continued)

SOURCE 2: Food poverty in the UK

MARKS

Monthly Bill	2013	2016	% change
Rent	£577	£594·31	3%
Council Tax	£92	£97·52	6%
Food	£256	£294·40	15%
Gas	£67	£81·74	22%
Electricity	£45	£54	20%
Phone line rental	£15	£13·50	−10%
Broadband	£17	£10·20	−40%
Total monthly spend	£1,069	£1,145·67	16%

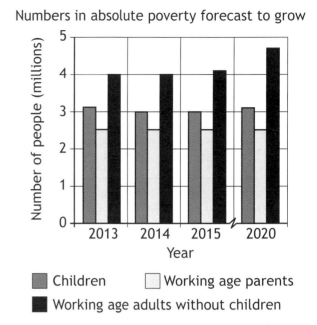

Numbers in absolute poverty forecast to grow

Children
Working age parents
Working age adults without children

SOURCE 3

Opinions about Foodbanks

Foodbank volunteer

Foodbanks are a useful emergency stopgap: the aim is that people should collect no more than three food parcels and after that there is support to figure out the real reason why they can't afford food. There is an increasing number of people who do not have enough to live on and many people rely on foodbanks when they are waiting for their benefit claims to be processed. People have been driven to desperate measures to get food.

Local police were criticised for giving foodbank vouchers to shoplifters but some people are so poor they had no choice but to turn to crime. It's true that some people abuse the system, spending their money on alcohol and tobacco, but these instances are few and far between.

Community representative

The growing availability of foodbanks causes their increase: if you provide a service, people will use it. Food from a foodbank is by definition free and there will be almost infinite demand. A local council spent over £240,000 on foodbanks but it would have been better spent on addiction clinics. It is essential that the government address the reasons why people rely on foodbanks whether it's addiction, alcoholism or mental illness.

In the longer term, we should be looking at improving the economy: we need to get people back to work, pay people better wages and improve the quality of apprenticeships. Schools have a role to play in making sure children are properly fed. There should be universal free school meals. Real help does not come in a food parcel.

Using Sources 1, 2 and 3, explain why the view of Greg Orr **is selective in the use of facts.**

> **Foodbanks are an effective solution to food poverty.**
>
> View of Greg Orr

In your answer you **must:**

- give evidence from the sources that supports Greg Orr's view

and

- give evidence from the sources that opposes Greg Orr's view.

Your answer **must** be based on all **three** sources.

8

NOW GO TO SECTION 3 ON PAGE 18

MARKS

PART D — CRIME AND THE LAW

In your answers to Questions 10 and 11 you should give recent examples from the United Kingdom.

Question 10

There are many consequences of crime on communities.

Describe, in **detail, two** consequences of crime on communities.

6

Question 11

Some people are more likely to commit crimes than others.

Explain, **in detail, two** reasons why some people are more likely to commit crime than others.

6

[Turn over for next question

DO NOT WRITE ON THIS PAGE

PART D (continued)

Question 12

Study Sources 1, 2 and 3 and then answer the question which follows.

SOURCE 1

Press Release — March 2016

Serious organised crime affects us all and we each have a part to play in reducing the harm it causes. It costs the Scottish economy and society billions of pounds each year and includes drugs, counterfeit goods, human trafficking and fraud.

Key Findings

- The Police find it very difficult to investigate and monitor communications. It is currently too easy for the key figures in organised crime to carry out their illegal activities online.

- Police Scotland has built partnerships with the public to tackle drugs crime and reduce the sale of counterfeit goods. Thousands of counterfeit CDs and DVDs have been seized during an intelligence led operation in Glasgow.

- The budget for Police Scotland needs to be increased from £1·1 billion to £1·3 billion to address the issues that have been raised concerning investigating organised crime.

- To improve performance, a government committee needs to be set up in order to investigate how Police Scotland can work with communication companies in their fight against organised crime.

- New offences have been introduced which has led to the conviction of those involved in organised crime. Police Scotland is cooperating much more with European organisations such as Europol to increase the exchange of intelligence to and from Scotland.

Number of Arrests for Organised Crime

Year	2013	2014	2015	2016
Arrests for organised crime	2078	2159	2342	2737

SOURCE 2

Selected Scottish Crime Statistics — (2013—2016)

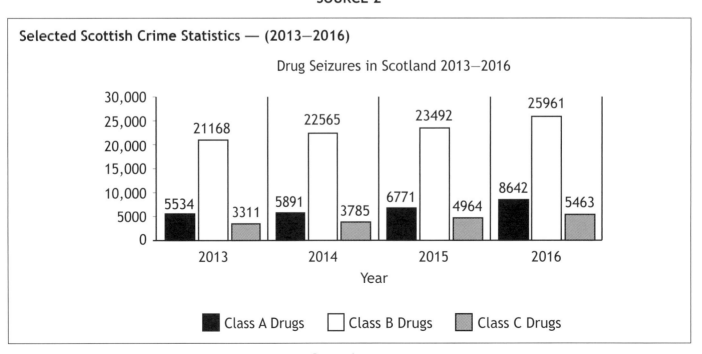

Drug Seizures in Scotland 2013—2016

Class A Drugs   Class B Drugs   Class C Drugs

PART D Question 12 Source 2 (continued)

MARKS

SOURCE 2

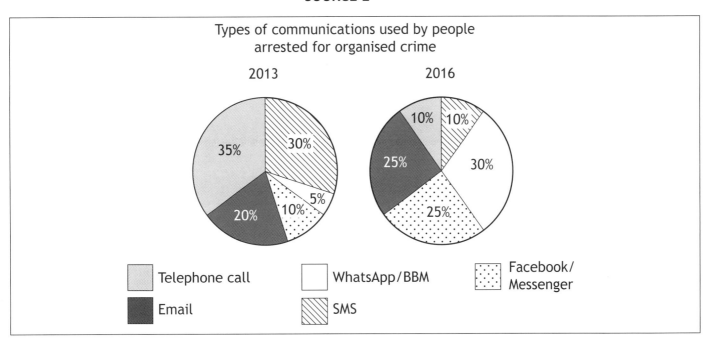

Types of communications used by people arrested for organised crime

SOURCE 3

Organised gangs using technology to evade police — News online

Organised criminals are using apps and encrypted messaging to avoid police, senior officers believe.

Criminals are now using apps, such as WhatsApp and BBM, which are based on their smart phones to contact each other. This means that they do not have itemised bills and it is much more difficult to trace and investigate them. Police Scotland has stated that even with these difficulties, they have increased the number of arrests in relation to organised crime.

Police Scotland is hindered by the strict guidelines imposed which limit the types of communication methods they have access to in an investigation. Senior officers believe most gangs are still profiting from "traditional" crimes but are using online resources to do deals and avoid detection, which makes organised crime so difficult to control.

The Scottish Government however has tried to help by tightening the laws surrounding what people can be prosecuted for in relation to organised crime. Police Scotland is also now working closely with HM Revenue and Customs and other European agencies to monitor and share information, in the fight against organised crime.

Using Sources 1, 2 and 3, explain why the view of Samara Ezra **is selective in the use of facts.**

Police Scotland is successfully tackling serious organised crime.

View of Samara Ezra

In your answer you must:

- give evidence from the sources that supports Samara Ezra's view

and

- give evidence from the sources that opposes Samara Ezra's view.

Your answer **must** be based on all **three** sources.

8

NOW GO TO SECTION 3 ON PAGE 18

MARKS

SECTION 3 — INTERNATIONAL ISSUES — 20 marks

Attempt ONE part, either

Part E — World Powers   on pages 18–21

OR

Part F — World Issues   on pages 22–25

PART E — WORLD POWERS

In your answers to Questions 13 and 14 you should give recent examples from a world power you have studied.

Question 13

There are many causes of socio-economic issues.

Describe, **in detail, two** causes of socio-economic issues in the world power you have studied.

In your answer you should state the world power you have studied.   **4**

Question 14

Some groups of people are less likely to participate in politics than others.

Explain, **in detail, two** reasons why some groups of people are less likely to participate in politics than others in the world power you have studied.

In your answer you should state the world power you have studied.   **6**

[Turn over for next question

DO NOT WRITE ON THIS PAGE

PART E (continued)

Question 15

Study Sources 1, 2 and 3 and then answer the question which follows.

You are an advisor at the European Union. You have been asked to recommend **whether or not** Serbia should be allowed to join the European Union.

Option 1	**Option 2**
Serbia should be allowed to join the European Union.	Serbia should not be allowed to join the European Union.

SOURCE 1

Becoming a member — The Copenhagen Criteria — a summary

Any European country can apply to be a member of the European Union (EU), if it respects the democratic values of the EU and is committed to promoting them. They also have to meet the EU's standards and rules, have the permission of the current EU members and finally they must have the approval of their citizens — shown in either their national parliament or by referendum.

The first step for any country that wishes to become a member, is meeting the Copenhagen Criteria.

The Copenhagen Criteria state that countries wishing to join the EU need to have:

- a stable democracy, the rule of law, human rights and respect for and protection of minorities;
- a stable economy and low unemployment;
- the ability to meet the conditions of membership effectively, both politically and financially.

Serbia's Progress to Date:
Serbia applied for full membership: December 2009 Confirmed as candidate: March 2012

Serbia's progress towards becoming a member of the EU was initially very slow, but EU leaders granted Serbia "candidate status" at a Brussels summit in March 2012. Serbia has since made significant progress in meeting the "Copenhagen Criteria". The EU is currently Serbia's biggest trading and investment partner. The government in Serbia is working well with the European Parliament to ensure all negotiating is running smoothly. Serbia has also recently become a member of the Western Balkan group and is forming relationships in their own region.

The European Council has however postponed negotiations with Serbia on two chapters of EU legislation after a complaint from the Croatian government, demanding better treatment of Croats in Serbia and more action on war crimes. Also human rights are still not as protected as they should be, with freedom of the media still a concern. In early July, a newspaper editor was severely beaten by three men who demanded money and were not happy about the newspaper's political views.

SOURCE 2

Media Coverage
Opinion Polls — Serbian Newspaper

Should Serbia be allowed to join the European Union?	Should Serbia form an alliance with Russia instead of the EU?
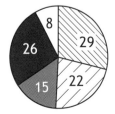	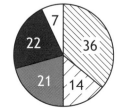

⧅ Strongly Agree   ◼ Strongly Disagree   ⧄ Agree   ▨ Disagree   ☐ Undecided

PART E Question 15 Source 2 (continued)

SOURCE 2   MARKS

UK Today

Serbia-Germany cooperation important for Serbia on the road to EU membership

The Star

CROATIA SUPPORTS EU ENLARGEMENT TO INCLUDE SERBIA, HAVING IN THE PAST BLOCKED IT

DAILY BLOG

Uncertainty for countries wishing to join the EU due to Brexit

The Mail Today

Greece, Bulgaria and Serbia meet to discuss the migrant crisis

SOURCE 3

<u>Country profile — Serbia</u>

There are currently over 7000 displaced refugees in Serbia from Syria. Serbia is finding it hard to cooperate with other members to help tackle the migrant crisis.

Many people in Serbia feel an alliance with Russia would be better for their economy rather than joining the EU.

Crime rates in Serbia are at an all-time low. There has been a large scale police crackdown on drugs this year and they have arrested 30 drug smugglers in a joint operation with Germany.

Floods in Serbia in 2014, had a negative impact on their economy. However, there was 3% growth of the Serbian economy in 2016.

<u>EU profile</u>

The European Union is currently made up of 28 countries. Great Britain has recently held a referendum to leave the European Union.

Many countries in the EU are getting worried about EU enlargement and do not want other countries to join.

The current members of the EU are worried about increasing political tension with Russia.

The EU has recently led peace talks between Kosovo and Serbia.

Migrants fleeing Syria are putting pressure on lots of members of the EU. This is causing conflict between members.

You must decide which option to recommend, **either** recommend Serbia should be allowed to join the European Union **(Option 1)** or recommend that Serbia should not be allowed to join the European Union **(Option 2)**.

(i)   Using Sources 1, 2 and 3, **which option would you choose**?

(ii) Give reasons to **support** your choice.

(iii) **Explain** why you did not choose the other option.

Your answer **must** be based on all **three** sources.   **10**

MARKS

PART F — WORLD ISSUES

In your answers to Questions 16 and 17 you should give recent examples from a world issue you have studied.

Question 16

> International issues and conflicts have many consequences.

Describe, **in detail, two** consequences of an international conflict or issue you have studied.

In your answer you should state the world issue or conflict you have studied.

4

Question 17

> International organisations have many reasons for attempting to resolve international issues and conflicts.

Selected International Organisations		
United Nations	NATO	European Union
Charities	African Union	NGOs

Select an International Organisation you have studied.

Explain, **in detail, two** reasons why it has attempted to resolve an international issue **or** conflict.

In your answer you should state the world issue or conflict you have studied.

6

[Turn over for next question

DO NOT WRITE ON THIS PAGE

PART F (continued)

Question 18

Study Sources 1, 2 and 3 and then answer the question which follows.

You are a government adviser. You have been asked to recommend **whether** or **not** Country Y should increase their minimum wage.

Option 1	**Option 2**
Increase minimum wage	Do not increase minimum wage

SOURCE 1

Country Y Factfile

Country Y is a country in Eastern Africa, with almost half the land used for farming. The average monthly wage in the country is twelve thousand shillings ($120), with the average hourly minimum wage currently 100 shillings ($1). However the average monthly wage for a farm worker is six thousand shillings ($60). The government of Country Y is currently considering increasing the hourly minimum wage by a further 10%.

- The population of Country Y is 43 million, with ethnic diversity providing a vibrant culture.

- Country Y has an unemployment rate of 40%. Many argue that this is a direct result of previous increases in the hourly minimum wage.

- The agricultural sector employs a large number of workers.

- Previous increases in minimum hourly wages have been viewed negatively by businesses as well as agricultural workers.

- 43% of the population of Country Y live below the poverty line, with more than 3 million people requiring food aid.

- Tourism played a significant role in bringing money into the country, however the country suffered a series of terrorist attacks during recent years which caused a huge decline in the number of foreign visitors.

- The risk of infectious disease in the country is high with 10% of the population living with HIV/AIDS.

- Television is the main news source in cities and towns. The spread of viewing in rural areas has been slower, hampered by limited access to mains electricity.

- The President of the country stated that an increase in pay should not simply be related to the cost of living but should be linked to the productivity of the workforce.

- Housing costs in Country Y are extremely high in relation to wages — on average, rents are seven thousand shillings ($70) per month and houses are often not equipped with proper sanitation facilities, which can lead to an increased risk of poor health.

SOURCE 2

Survey of working age population

Should the government
increase the minimum wage?

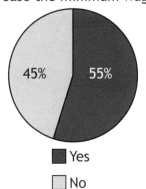

Should the government introduce income
support rather than minimum wage?

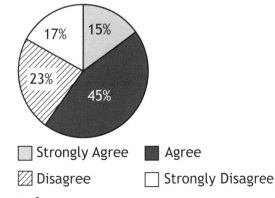

■ Yes
☐ No

☐ Strongly Agree   ■ Agree
▨ Disagree   ☐ Strongly Disagree

PART F Question 18 Source 2 (continued)   MARKS

SOURCE 2

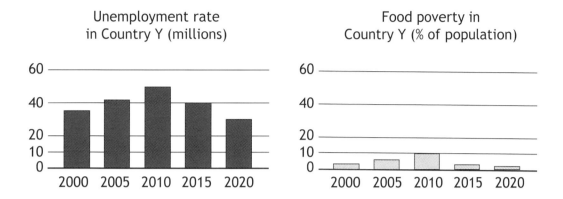

Unemployment rate in Country Y (millions)

Food poverty in Country Y (% of population)

SOURCE 3

Viewpoints

Our members have campaigned tirelessly for an increase of 20% on the hourly minimum wage as we feel 10% is not enough. Members continually highlight how many workers have little money left after paying housing costs for the month. This affects how much money families have to spend on food and education for their children.

Current low wages also restrict accessing medical treatment when required as it is simply unaffordable. Many families report that they cannot afford to pay for vaccinations for their children or access the correct medication to treat illnesses such as HIV and AIDS. It is vital that the government acts quickly.

Local Trade Union Member

The government, 3 years ago, increased the minimum hourly wage by 14%. This had a major impact on businesses as well as agricultural workers. We often suffer droughts, as well as flooding during the rainy season, and with little produce to sell we can barely afford to survive ourselves never mind pay our workers more money.

A further increase in the minimum wage will result in greater unemployment, which will be a bigger issue for the government to deal with. The government must hold discussions with employers as well as the trade unions to negotiate a deal that will benefit everyone.

Local Farmer

You must decide which option to recommend, **either** increase minimum wage **(Option 1)** or do not increase minimum wage **(Option 2)**.

(i) Using Sources 1, 2 and 3, **which option would you choose?**

(ii) Give reasons to **support** your choice.

(iii) **Explain** why you did not choose the other option.

Your answer **must** be based on all **three** sources.   10

[END OF QUESTION PAPER]

[BLANK PAGE]

DO NOT WRITE ON THIS PAGE

NATIONAL 5

2017 Specimen Question Paper

National Qualifications 2017

S849/75/11

Modern Studies

Date — Not applicable

Duration — 2 hours 20 minutes

Total marks — 80

SECTION 1 — DEMOCRACY IN SCOTLAND AND THE UNITED KINGDOM — 28 marks

Attempt **EITHER** Part A **AND** Question 7 **OR** Part B **AND** Question 7

SECTION 2 — SOCIAL ISSUES IN THE UNITED KINGDOM — 26 marks

Attempt **EITHER** Part C **AND** Question 14 **OR** Part D **AND** Question 14

SECTION 3 — INTERNATIONAL ISSUES — 26 marks

Attempt **EITHER** Part E **AND** Question 21 **OR** Part F **AND** Question 21

Write your answers clearly in the answer booklet provided. In the answer booklet you must clearly identify the question number you are attempting.

Use **blue** or **black** ink.

Before leaving the examination room you must give your answer booklet to the Invigilator; if you do not, you may lose all the marks for this paper.

MARKS

SECTION 1 — DEMOCRACY IN SCOTLAND AND THE UNITED KINGDOM — 28 marks

Attempt **EITHER** Part A **AND** Question 7 **OR** Part B **AND** Question 7

Part A	Democracy in Scotland	Pages 02-03
Part B	Democracy in the United Kingdom	Pages 04-05
Question 7		Pages 06-07

PART A — DEMOCRACY IN SCOTLAND

In your answers to Questions 1, 2 and 3 you should give recent examples from Scotland.

Question 1

> In Scottish Parliament elections, political parties campaign in many ways.

Describe, **in detail**, **two** ways that political parties campaign in Scottish Parliament elections.

4

Question 2

> The Scottish Parliament has responsibility for devolved matters.

Describe, **in detail**, **two** devolved matters for which the Scottish Parliament has responsibility.

6

Attempt **EITHER** Question 3(a) **OR** 3(b) on *Page three*

MARKS

Attempt **EITHER** Question 3(a) **OR** 3(b)

Question 3

(a)

> The Additional Member System (AMS) has several advantages.

Explain, **in detail**, the advantages of the Additional Member System (AMS).

You should give a **maximum** of **three** advantages in your answer.   **8**

OR

(b)

> People in Scotland can participate in society in many ways.

Explain, **in detail**, why some people in Scotland participate in one of the following:

- Pressure Groups
- Trade Unions.

You should give a **maximum** of **three** reasons in your answer.   **8**

[Now go to Question 7 starting on *Page six*]

MARKS

PART B — DEMOCRACY IN THE UNITED KINGDOM

In your answers to Questions 4, 5 and 6 you should give recent examples from the United Kingdom.

Question 4

> In General Elections, political parties campaign in many ways.

Describe, **in detail, two** ways political parties campaign during General Elections.   **4**

Question 5

> The UK Parliament has responsibility for reserved matters in Scotland.

Describe, **in detail**, **two** reserved matters for which the UK Parliament has responsibility.   **6**

Attempt **EITHER** Question 6(a) **OR** 6(b) **on** *Page five*

MARKS

Attempt **EITHER** Question 6(a) **OR** 6(b)

Question 6

(a)

First Past the Post has several disadvantages.

Explain, **in detail,** the disadvantages of First Past the Post.

You should give a **maximum** of **three** disadvantages in your answer.   8

OR

(b)

People in the UK can participate in society in many ways.

Explain, **in detail**, why some people in the UK participate in one of the following:

- Pressure Groups
- Trade Unions.

You should give a **maximum** of **three** reasons in your answer.   8

[Now go to Question 7 starting on *Page six*]

Question 7

Study Sources 1, 2 and 3 and then answer the question which follows.

SOURCE 1

Composition of the House of Lords

The House of Commons and the House of Lords make up the two Chambers in the UK Parliament. In recent years, some changes have been made to the composition of the Lords. In 1995, over half of those who sat in the House of Lords were hereditary peers (this means they inherited their seat in the Lords from their father). The total number of Lords has changed and currently there are about 790 members, none of whom are directly elected by the public.

By 1997, about 36% of the House of Lords were appointed as a Lord for the length of their life (a life peer). Today, approximately 90% of Lords are life peers. Many Lords bring great experience and expertise to Parliament in the fields of medicine, law, business, science, sport and education, to name a few areas.

Although women have only been allowed to sit in the House of Lords since 1958, the Lord Speaker's role which was created in 2006 was initially held by two female peers, Baroness Hayman (2006-2011) and Baroness D'Souza (2011-2016). It is the Lord Speaker's job to oversee the business in the House of Lords. Lord Fowler, the current Lord Speaker, became the first man to occupy the position in 2016.

In the House of Lords, since 2000, 36% of newly appointed members have been women, 21% have been ethnic minorities and 10% have been disabled.

SOURCE 2

Comparison of selected factors in the House of Lords and the UK population

	House of Lords		UK population	
	1995	2015	1995	2015
Male	93%	75%	49%	49%
Female	7%	25%	51%	51%
Ethnic-minority background	Less than 1%	5%	6%	13%
% under 60 years of age	22%	16%	81%	77%
Average age	79	70	36	40
Privately educated	62%	50%	7%	7%
Graduated from Oxford or Cambridge University	35%	38%	Less than 1%	Less than 1%
Disabled	2%	11%	12%	17%

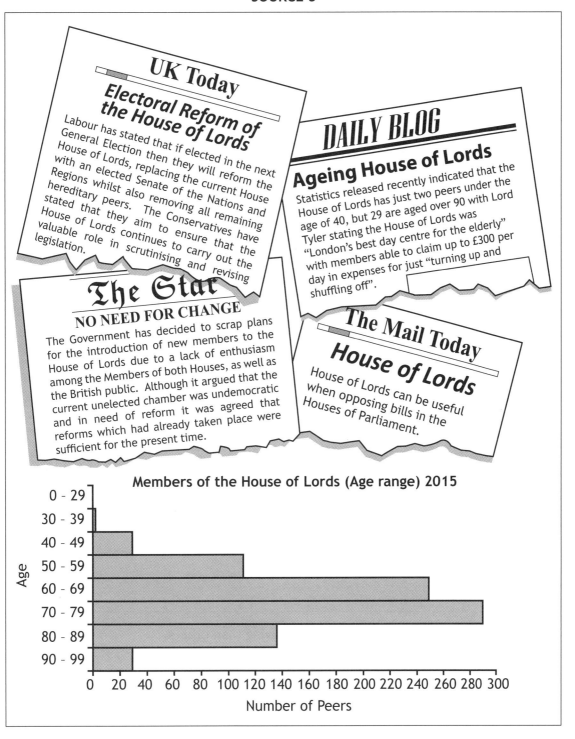

UK Today

Electoral Reform of the House of Lords

Labour has stated that if elected in the next General Election then they will reform the House of Lords, replacing the current House with an elected Senate of the Nations and Regions whilst also removing all remaining hereditary peers. The Conservatives have stated that they aim to ensure that the House of Lords continues to carry out the valuable role in scrutinising and revising legislation.

DAILY BLOG

Ageing House of Lords

Statistics released recently indicated that the House of Lords has just two peers under the age of 40, but 29 are aged over 90 with Lord Tyler stating the House of Lords was "London's best day centre for the elderly" with members able to claim up to £300 per day in expenses for just "turning up and shuffling off".

The Star

NO NEED FOR CHANGE

The Government has decided to scrap plans for the introduction of new members to the House of Lords due to a lack of enthusiasm among the Members of both Houses, as well as the British public. Although it argued that the current unelected chamber was undemocratic and in need of reform it was agreed that reforms which had already taken place were sufficient for the present time.

The Mail Today

House of Lords

House of Lords can be useful when opposing bills in the Houses of Parliament.

Members of the House of Lords (Age range) 2015

Using Sources 1, 2 and 3, explain why the view of Morag Watt **is selective in the use of facts.**

> The House of Lords is in need of further reform.
>
> **View of Morag Watt**

In your answer you **must:**

- give evidence from the sources that supports Morag Watt's view

and

- give evidence from the sources that opposes Morag Watt's view.

Your answer **must** be based on all **three** sources.

10

NOW GO TO SECTION 2 ON *Page eight*

SECTION 2 – SOCIAL ISSUES IN THE UNITED KINGDOM – 26 marks   MARKS

Attempt **EITHER** Part C **AND** Question 14 **OR** Part D **AND** Question 14

Part C   Social Inequality   Page 8

Part D   Crime and the Law   Page 9

Question 14   Pages 10–11

PART C – SOCIAL INEQUALITY

In your answers to Questions 8, 9 and 10 you should give recent examples from the United Kingdom.

Question 8

Groups that experience inequality in the UK		
Women	Ethnic Minorities	Elderly

Choose **one** of the groups above **or any other group** you have studied.

Describe, **in detail**, **two** ways the Government has tried to reduce the inequalities experienced by the group you have chosen.   4

Question 9

Some people in the UK have a better standard of living than others.

Explain, **in detail**, **two** reasons why some people in the UK have a better standard of living than others.   6

Question 10

There are many groups in the UK which experience social and economic inequality.

Explain, **in detail**, **two** reasons why one or more groups you have studied experience social and economic inequality in the UK.   6

[Now go to Question 14 starting on *Page ten*]

MARKS

PART D – CRIME AND THE LAW

In your answers to Questions 11, 12 and 13 you should give recent examples from the United Kingdom.

Question 11

Groups that tackle crime in the UK		
Government	Police	Courts

Choose **one** of the groups above.

Describe, **in detail**, **two** ways in which the group you have chosen has tried to tackle crime in the UK.   4

Question 12

Some people are affected by crime more than others.

Explain, **in detail**, **two** reasons why some people are affected by crime more than others.   6

Question 13

There are many factors which cause crime in the UK.

Explain, **in detail**, **two** factors which cause crime in the UK.   6

[Now go to Question 14 starting on *Page ten*]

Question 14

Study Sources 1, 2 and 3 and then answer the question which follows.

You are a government adviser. You have been asked to recommend **whether** or **not** the United Kingdom Government should ban Legal Highs.

Option 1	**Option 2**
Ban Legal Highs	Do not ban Legal Highs

SOURCE 1

Legal Highs Factfile

The UK Government is currently examining legislation that will control the sale and use of "legal highs". A legal high contains one or more chemical substances which produce similar effects to illegal drugs, like cocaine, cannabis and ecstasy. These drugs are often included in everyday household products and are often labelled "not for human consumption". Legal highs are often seen as "designer drugs" and can be easily bought and sold online.

- Legal highs are currently not covered by the Misuse of Drugs Act, 1971.
- Some EU countries have already passed legislation controlling the sale and use of legal highs.
- There was a mass demonstration against the proposed legislation due to the inclusion of nitrous oxide, otherwise known as laughing gas, within the bill. Nitrous oxide is commonly used as an anaesthetic during dentistry, childbirth and as a mood enhancer.
- Legal highs have been linked to hospital admissions for things such as poisoning, mental health issues, and in extreme cases death.
- Despite the media attention, around half of young people have never experimented with legal highs.
- The government is looking at a bill that will make it illegal to sell any "psychoactive substances" other than alcohol, caffeine and nicotine.
- There has been little or no research into the long term or short term risks of taking legal highs.
- The UK has the most severe problem with legal highs in Western Europe, with significant numbers of young people regularly admitting to taking legal highs.
- Many health experts argue banning legal highs will not prevent people taking them; educating people on the danger of these substances would be more beneficial.
- Under the proposed legislation, possession will remain legal so long as there is no intent to supply. The bill could mean up to seven years in prison for people who provide drugs to others.

SOURCE 2

Survey of 16-25 year olds on legal highs

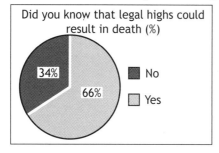

Did you know that legal highs could result in death (%)

34% No
66% Yes

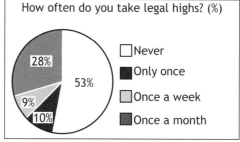

How often do you take legal highs? (%)

Never
Only once
Once a week
Once a month

28%
53%
9%
10%

MARKS

Question 14 (continued)

SOURCE 2 (continued)

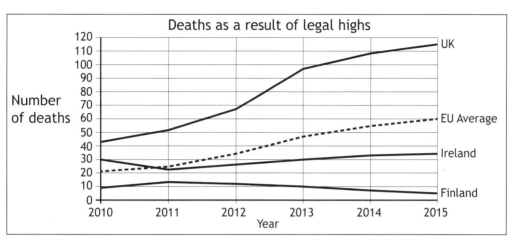

SOURCE 3

Viewpoints

Control and monitoring of legal highs is very difficult. Current laws mean that decisions on whether a product is allowed to be sold are made on a case by case basis. Often new versions are created and sold just as fast as the government can ban them. This makes it difficult to monitor and police.

The government's plan for a blanket ban on legal highs is impractical and not supported by everyone. The Irish government banned legal highs after a number of deaths linked to their use; however this did not reduce deaths and was unsuccessful.

Anna Drummond, Youth Worker

More of my time as a paramedic is being taken up dealing with the consequences of legal highs. The misuse of these drugs diverts our attention from cases that are much more important.

Legal highs are becoming increasingly popular particularly among young people who assume "legal" means "safe". Young people have become much more aware of the health risks of illegal drugs and we see fewer young people addicted to drugs like heroin. However, lots of people are unaware of the dangers of legal highs.

Mandeep Khan, Paramedic

You must decide which option to recommend, **either** ban Legal Highs (**Option 1**) **or** do not ban Legal Highs (**Option 2**).

  (i)   Using Sources 1, 2 and 3, **which option would you choose**?

 (ii)   Give reasons to **support** your choice.

(iii)   **Explain** why you did not choose the other option.

Your answer must be based on all **three** sources.

10

NOW GO TO SECTION 3 ON *Page twelve*

SECTION 3 — INTERNATIONAL ISSUES — 26 marks   MARKS

Attempt **EITHER** Part E **AND** Question 21 **OR** Part F **AND** Question 21

Part E   World Powers   Page 12

Part F   World Issues   Page 13

Question 21   Pages 14–15

PART E — WORLD POWERS

In your answers to Questions 15, 16 and 17 you should give recent examples from a world power you have studied.

Question 15

Governments have made many attempts to tackle social and economic inequality.

Describe, **in detail**, **two** ways in which the government has tried to tackle social and economic inequality.

In your answer you must state the world power you have studied.   4

Question 16

The citizens of every world power have political rights.

Describe, **in detail**, **two** political rights that the citizens have in the world power you have studied.

In your answer you must state the world power you have studied.   6

Question 17

World powers have the ability to influence other countries.

Explain, **in detail**, **two** reasons why the world power you have studied has the ability to influence other countries.

In your answer you must state the world power you have studied.   6

[Now go to Question 21 starting on *Page fourteen*]

PART F — WORLD ISSUES

In your answers to Questions 18, 19 and 20 you should give recent examples from a world issue you have studied.

Question 18

International organisations which try to resolve international issues and problems		
United Nations Organisation	NATO	World Bank
European Union	African Union	Charities and other NGOs

Describe, **in detail**, **two** ways in which international organisations have tried to resolve an international issue or conflict you have studied.

In your answer you must state the world issue or conflict you have studied.　**4**

Question 19

People are affected by international conflicts and issues in many different ways.

Describe, **in detail**, **two** ways in which people have been affected by an international conflict or issue you have studied.

In your answer you must state the world issue or conflict you have studied.　**6**

Question 20

The attempts of international organisations to tackle conflicts and issues are sometimes unsuccessful.

Explain, **in detail**, **two** reasons why international organisations have **either** been successful **or** unsuccessful in tackling an international conflict or issue you have studied.

In your answer you must state the world issue or conflict you have studied.　**6**

[Now go to Question 21 starting on *Page fourteen*]

Question 21

Study Sources 1, 2 and 3 and then answer the question which follows.

SOURCE 1

Problems facing Japan in 2015

Many people think Japan is in crisis. Its problems include a weak economy and a rapidly changing population structure. All of these things are long term problems which are affecting Japanese standards of living.

Since the economic crisis that hit the world in 2008, low incomes have become a problem. It is estimated that 16% of all Japanese people are living below the poverty line. Average income went from 37,185 US dollars in 2008 to 34,822 US dollars in 2011.

One third of working age women now live in poverty. 12 million women in Japan work but over half are in part-time jobs, receiving small salaries. Part-time work helps those with families and school-age children but has a negative impact because it prevents many from having financial savings which is a major worry for Japanese women.

Increased poverty and a different population structure will make old age pensions and elderly care very expensive in the future. By the middle of this century over one third of the population will be collecting their old age pension.

Despite all the problems facing modern Japan, many people point to its strengths. It had 22 crimes per 1,000 people in 2014. It remains the third largest economy in the world where some people still enjoy an extremely high standard of living.

SOURCE 2

Additional statistics - Selected Countries				
	People in poverty (%)	Crimes per 1000 people	Home ownership (%)	Internet access per 1000 people
Germany	15	79	44	841
Argentina	30	36	67	599
South Korea	16·5	32	54	865
Italy	19·6	39	74	585
France	8	61	64	819
European Union	8	80	71	848

MARKS

SOURCE 2 (continued)

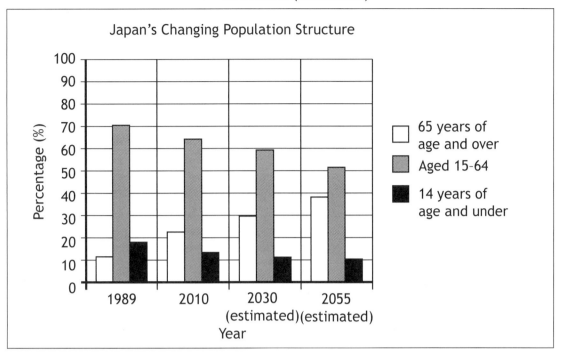

Japan's Changing Population Structure

Legend:
- 65 years of age and over
- Aged 15-64
- 14 years of age and under

SOURCE 3

Better Life Index Study

According to the Better Life Index, citizens in Japan are not entirely happy.

Japanese women have an average happiness level of 4·67 (out of 10) whereas Japanese men have an average level of 6·21. However, happiness is not equal amongst all women. Working age women have a happiness level of 3·2 whilst 70-74 year olds have a level of 5·5.

Japan boasts one of the highest life expectancies in the world at 83 years. In future this may be difficult to maintain as the proportion of the population paying tax falls.

The country continues to be at the forefront of the electronics industry which employs many people. Of every 1000 Japanese people, 865 have access to the internet. Just over three quarters of Japanese people say they are satisfied with their home. 61% of Japanese people own their own homes but housing has become much more expensive for young people due to the growing numbers of older people.

Using Sources 1, 2 and 3, what **conclusions** can be drawn?

You should reach a conclusion about each of the following:

- The problem of crime in Japan compared to other countries.
- The effects of the changing population structure in Japan.
- The effect of poverty on working age women.
- The country most like Japan.

Your conclusions must be supported by evidence from the sources. You should link information within and between the sources in support of your conclusions.

Your answer **must** be based on all **three** sources.

10

[END OF SPECIMEN QUESTION PAPER]

NATIONAL 5

Answers

NATIONAL 5 MODERN STUDIES 2015

Section 1

Part A: Democracy in Scotland

1. *Candidates can be credited in a number of ways up to a maximum of 4 marks.*

   Possible approaches to answering the question:

   Councils provide services such as education.
   [1 mark – accurate but undeveloped point]

   Councils provide services such as education. They provide education from 3–18 in schools.
   [2 marks – accurate with development]

   Dundee City is one of Scotland's 32 local councils. Education is a key service. Nurseries, primary and secondary schools are all funded by the Council. They employ the teachers and people such as janitors to provide the service.
   [3 marks – accurate point with development and detailed exemplification]

   Credit reference to aspects of the following:

   Some pupils may refer to the types of services and should be credited for this.

   Mandatory services – such as schooling for 5–16 year olds, social work services.

   Discretionary services – swimming pools, mobile libraries.

   Permissive powers such as economic development, recreation services; and,

   Regulatory powers – Local Authorities provide regulatory services such as trading standards and environmental health and issue licences for taxis and public houses.

   Councils deliver a wide range of valuable services to their local area. The main services they provide, in addition to their regulatory and licensing functions, are:
   • Education
   • Social Work
   • Roads and transport
   • Economic Development
   • Housing and the Built Environment
   • The Environment
   • Libraries
   • Waste management
   • Arts, Culture and Sport

   Councils also work with external agencies such as the police and fire service to provide community safety.

   Any other valid point that meets the criteria described in the general marking instructions for this kind of question.

2. *Candidates can be credited in a number of ways up to a maximum of 6 marks.*

   Possible approaches to answering the question:

   People may choose to use the media to influence people.
   [1 mark – accurate but undeveloped point]

   People may join a trade union to protect their rights at work eg teachers join the EIS.
   [2 marks – accurate with development]

   People may join a trade union to protect their rights at work eg teachers join the EIS. They might do this because they feel that they are not getting paid enough money and that the union will take action for them eg talking to their employers.
   [3 marks – accurate point with development and exemplification]

   People may choose to join a pressure group such as Greenpeace because they are worried about the environment and they feel they can't make any difference on their own. Joining a pressure group means lots of people campaign together so they have more of an impact eg Greenpeace have 11,000 Scottish members, this gives them strength in numbers and increases their collective influence on the government. This makes them difficult to ignore.
   [4 marks – relevant accurate point with development, analysis and exemplification]

   Credit reference to aspects of the following:

   Pressure Groups
   • Believe strongly about an issue such as human rights, the environment.
   • Collective action more effective than individual.
   • Media pay more attention to organised pressure groups.
   • Pressure groups have experience of campaigning etc.
   • Seen as the best way to influence government in between elections.

   Trade Unions
   • Protect rights at work eg health and safety, pay, holidays, pensions.
   • TU have experience negotiating with management.
   • TU have legal teams you can use.
   • Collective action more effective than individual.

   The Media
   • Use them to get wider attention for an issue you care about eg newspapers are widely read.
   • Legal way to get attention for your cause.
   • Local and national appeal.
   • Use of different media types eg Facebook campaigns.

3. *Candidates can be credited in a number of ways up to a maximum of 10 marks.*

   Possible approaches to answering the question:

   For Option 1:

   I would choose Daisy as she has experience as a councillor.
   [1 mark – evidence drawn from Source 1]

   In Source 1 Daisy says that health needs to improve as lives are being cut short. She is right as life expectancy is less in Glenlochy.
   [2 marks – evaluative terminology with limited evidence from Source 1 and Source 2]

   In Source 1 Daisy states that "The lives of people in Glenlochy are being cruelly cut short". She is correct as Source 2 states life expectancy is only 77 years compared to 79 in the rest of Scotland, a significant difference of two years.
   [3 marks – evidence drawn from two Sources with detailed use of evidence and evaluative terminology]

   Reference to aspects of the following will be credited:
   • Local Councillor [Source 1] – constituents want an experienced politician [Source 2].

- Source 1 – "I will work to ensure that more women are elected" Source 2 – 54% agree.
- 54% think the Scottish parliament needs more female MSPs [Source 2] and Daisy as a female would be a good choice [Source 1].
- Source 1 – number of women working locally – Source 3 – only 34% in Glenlochy but 45% in Scotland.
- Source 1 – unemployment a problem – true as 9% unemployed in Glenlochy and 7% in Scotland [Source 3].
- Childcare is a problem [Source 1] – 68% in Source 2 agree.

Against Option 1

Daisy claims a lack of internet access is an obvious barrier however Source 3 shows 3% more households in Glenlochy have access to the internet [2 marks].

Reference to aspects of the following will be credited:
- A lack of internet access [Source 1] – but Source 3 shows 79% have access compared to 76% in Scotland.
- Crime is not a concern [Source 1] but Source 2 shows 530 people attended a local meeting and raised valid concerns.
- Crime is not a concern [Source 1] Source 2 – 65% disagree with her.
- Daisy says health needs to improve but there are fewer long-term illnesses in Glenlochy, 3% less than the UK [Source 3].
- Community council say a legal background is necessary [Source 2] but Daisy doesn't have this [Source 1].

For Option 2:

I would choose Tom because he has experience as a lawyer and Source 2 says our new MSPs should have a legal background.
[2 marks – evidence drawn from Sources 1 and 2]

Tom says that employment is a key issue which has to be improved [Source1]. He is right as Source 3 shows that unemployment is higher in Glenlochy.
[2 marks – evidence drawn from Sources 1 and 3]

In Source 1 – Tom says that "Too few people are in full-time work. He is right as Glenlochy's full-time employment rate is 6% lower than the rest of Scotland according to Source 3. This is clearly a problem, especially as according to Source 2 there is only one major employer in the local area and it recently made 100 people redundant.
[3 marks – evidence drawn from 3 Sources with detailed use of evidence and evaluative terminology]

Reference to aspects of the following will be credited:
- Source 1 – Tom is a lawyer and Source 2 – local people worried about crime would like an MSP with a legal background.
- Source 1 – too few people are in full-time work and Source 3 shows only 42% working compared to 48%.
- Source 1 – many relying on benefits and Source 3 shows 1.7% more claimants in Glenlochy compared to Scotland as whole.
- Source 1 – crime is a major concern and Source 2 shows 530 people attended a meeting to voice concerns.
- Source 1 – crime is a major concern and Source 2 shows 65% of people agree it's a problem.

Against Option 2

Tom claims that a lack of childcare isn't a problem in Glenlochy but 68% of local people think it is a major problem [2 marks].

Reference to aspects of the following will be credited:
- "The majority of local people agree with me that elderly people are well cared for" [Source 1] but Source 2 shows only 35% agree.

- Childcare not a problem [Source 1] – Source 2 68% feel it is.
- Tom says too many are leaving school before S6 [Source 1] – this isn't the case according to Source 3 – 2% more stay to S6 than the Scottish average.
- Many feel Glenlochy needs an experience representative [Source 2] and Tom has no experience as a representative [Source 1].

Part B: Democracy in the United Kingdom

4. *Candidates can be credited in a number of ways up to a maximum of 4 marks.*

Possible approaches to answering the question:

They examine government decisions.
[1 mark – accurate but undeveloped point]

The Lords can delay government bills by a year if they disagree.
[2 marks – accurate with development]

The Lords can contribute to government decision making as some of them can hold positions in the Cabinet and attend Cabinet meetings eg Baroness Stowell. Members of the House of Lords have been appointed to other government posts in recent years.
[3 marks – accurate point with development and exemplification]

Credit reference to aspects of the following:
- Provides detailed scrutiny and discussion of legislation due to experience and expertise of members.
- Can amend or reject legislation (limited by Parliament Acts).
- Can introduce bills (not money bills).
- May be able to force government to rethink legislation or policy as opposition in the Lords is often bad publicity for the government.
- Peers can be appointed as government ministers and some do attend full cabinet meetings.

5. *Candidates can be credited in a number of ways up to a maximum of 6 marks.*

Possible approaches to answering the question:

People may choose to use the media to influence people.
[1 mark – accurate but undeveloped point]

People may join a trade union to protect their rights at work eg rail workers join the Rail, Maritime and Transport Union (RMT).
[2 marks – accurate with development]

People may join a trade union to protect their rights at work eg rail workers join the Rail, Maritime and Transport Union (RMT). They might do this because they feel that they are not getting paid enough money and that the union will take action for them eg talking to their employers.
[3 marks – accurate point with development and exemplification]

People may choose to join a pressure group such as Greenpeace because they are worried about the environment and they feel they can't make any difference on their own. Joining a pressure group means lots of people campaign together so they have more of an impact eg Greenpeace have 130,000 UK supporters, this gives them strength in numbers and increases their collective influence on the government. This makes them difficult to ignore.
[4 marks – relevant accurate point with development, analysis and exemplification]

Credit reference to aspects of the following:

Pressure Groups
- Believe strongly about an issue such as human rights, the environment.
- Collective action more effective than individual.
- Media pay more attention to organised pressure groups.
- Pressure groups have experience of campaigning etc.
- Seen as the best way to influence government in between elections.

Trades Unions
- Protect rights at work eg health and safety, pay, holidays, pensions.
- TU have experience negotiating with management.
- TU have legal teams you can use.
- Collective action more effective than individual.

The Media
- Use them to get wider attention for an issue you care about eg newspapers are widely read.
- Legal way to get attention for your cause.
- Local and national appeal.
- Use of different media types eg Facebook campaigns.

6. *Candidates can be credited in a number of ways **up to a maximum of 10 marks**.*

Possible approaches to answering the question:

OPTION 1

For Option 1:

I would choose Nora as she has experience as a councillor.
[1 mark – evidence drawn from Source 1]

In Source 1 Nora says that health needs to improve as lives are being cut short. She is right as life expectancy is less in Millwood.
[2 marks – evaluative terminology with limited evidence from Source 1 and Source 2]

In Source 1 Nora states that "The lives of people in Millwood are being cruelly cut short". She is correct as Source 2 states life expectancy is only 77 years compared to 80 in the rest of the UK, a significant difference of three years.
[3 marks – evidence drawn from 2 Sources with detailed use of evidence and evaluative terminology]

Reference to aspects of the following will be credited:
- Local Councillor [Source 1] – constituents want an experienced politician [Source 2].
- Source 1 – more women are elected – Source 2 54% agree.
- Source 1 – number of women working locally – Source 3 only 34% in Millwood but 45% in UK.
- Source 1 – unemployment a problem; true as 9% unemployed in Millwood and 6% in UK [Source 3].
- Childcare is a problem [Source 1] and 68% in Source 2 agree.

Against Option 1

Nora claims a lack of internet access is an obvious barrier however Source 3 shows 2% more households in Millwood have access to the internet [2 marks].

Reference to aspects of the following will be credited:
- Source 1 – a lack of internet access Source 1 – but Source 3 shows 79% have access compared to 77% in UK.
- Source 1 – crime is not a problem but Source 2 shows 530 people attended a local meeting and raised valid concerns.
- Source 1 – crime is not a problem – Source 2 – 61% disagree with Nora.

- Nora says health needs to improve but there are fewer long-term illnesses in Millwood, 3% less than the UK [Source 3].
- Community council say a legal background [Source 2] is necessary but Nora doesn't have this [Source 1].

For Option 2:

I would choose John because he is a lawyer and Source 2 says our new MP should have a legal background.
[2 marks – evidence drawn from Sources 1 and 2]

John says that employment is a key issue which has to be improved (Source1). He is right as Source 3 shows 9% of Millwood are unemployed compared to 6% of UK.
[2 marks – evidence drawn from Sources 1 and 3]

In Source 1 John says that "Too few people are in full-time work. He is right as Millwood's full-time employment rate is 7% lower than the UK's.

This is clearly a problem, especially as according to Source 2 there is only one major employer in the local area and it recently made 100 people redundant.
[3 marks – evidence drawn from 3 Sources with detailed use of evidence and evaluative terminology]

Reference to aspects of the following will be credited:
- Source 1 – John is a lawyer and Source 2 shows local people are worried about crime and would like an MP with a legal background.
- Source 1 – too few people are in full-time work and Source 3 shows only 42% working compared to 49%.
- Source 1 – too many relying on benefits – Source 3 shows 2.3% more claimants in Millwood.
- Source 1 – crime is a major concern and Source 2 shows 530 people attended a meeting to voice concerns.
- Source 1 – crime is a major concern and 61% of people agree it's a problem [Source 2].

Against Option 2

John claims that a lack of childcare isn't a problem in Millwood but 68% of local people think it is a major problem [2 marks].

Reference to aspects of the following will be credited:
- The majority agree elderly are well cared for but Source 2 shows only 35% agree.
- Childcare not a problem – Source 2 68% feel it is.
- John says too many are leaving school before S6 – this isn't the case according to Source 3 – 3% more stay to S6 than the UK average.

Section 2

Part C: Social Inequality

7. *Candidates can be credited in a number of ways **up to a maximum of 4 marks**.*

Possible approaches to answering the question:

The Government has tried to reduce social inequalities by encouraging people to make better lifestyle choices.
[1 mark – accurate but undeveloped point]

The Government has tried to reduce social inequalities in housing by providing Social Housing to those who need it, to make sure everyone has an acceptable standard of housing.
[2 marks – accurate with development]

The Government has tried to reduce social inequalities in education by providing free state education. They also reduce inequalities within education by providing free school meals and clothing vouchers to pupils from lower income backgrounds.

[3 marks – accurate point with development and exemplification]

Credit reference to aspects of the following:

- **Health:** Passing Laws, providing free health care, issuing public guidelines (smoking/exercise/healthy eating).
- **Education:** Educational Maintenance Allowance (EMA); Student Loans; Scholarships and bursaries.
- **Housing:** Housing benefit.
- **Discrimination:** Equality Act 2010, Equality & Human Rights Commission (EHRC).
- **Welfare Benefits:** the government provides a huge range of benefits for the elderly, families, out of work, disabled etc.

8. *Candidates can be credited in a number of ways* **up to a maximum of 8 marks.**

Possible approaches to answering the question:

Ethnic minorities still face inequality in society because they still face racism in some areas of society.

[1 mark – accurate but undeveloped point]

Older people still face inequality in society because they face discrimination in the world of work because some employers think they don't have IT skills.

[2 marks – accurate with development]

Women still face inequality in society because of sexism. Employers, for example, might not want to employ a woman as they think she will need time off to look after her children. This means that women find it more difficult to find suitable work and as a result often work part-time in occupations like cleaning, childcare etc. Many women feel that the glass ceiling still exists which limits opportunities for promotion in their careers.

[4 marks – accurate point with development, analysis and exemplification]

Credit reference to aspects of the following:

- **Ethnic Minorities:** Prejudice, language barriers, poor educational attainment, higher unemployment rates, specific health issues.
- **Older People:** Ageism; financial preparation for retirement; previous occupation; family support; changes to benefit system, ie bedroom tax and employability.
- **Women:** Sexism; glass ceiling; pay gap; employment in 5C's, childcare availability and costs.
- **Disabled:** Prejudice; over qualification; lack of work experience; family support network; continuing health issues; reliance on benefits.
- **Lone Parents:** Prejudice, family commitments, lack of qualifications, no support network/childcare.
- **Unemployed:** Stigma of long-term unemployment, lack of experience,
- Changes to the benefit system, the recession.

9. *Candidates can be credited in a number of ways* **up to a maximum of 8 marks.**

Possible approaches to answering the question:

The impact of poverty on a child's life

Conclusion – Poverty can have a big impact on a child's health.

[1 mark – valid conclusion]

Poverty can have a big impact on a child's health. [1 mark – valid conclusion] For example, life expectancy for the poorest children is only 71 years [Source 2].

[2 marks – conclusion and evidence from one source]

Conclusion – Poverty can have a big impact on many areas of a child's life [1 mark valid conclusion]. Children living in poverty find themselves socially excluded from everyday life [Source 1]. Sixty two per cent of poor families cannot afford a week's holiday compared to only 6% of wealthy families [Source 2].

[3 marks – conclusion and information from two sources]

Conclusion – Poverty can have a big impact on many areas of a child's health. [1 mark valid conclusion] This is backed up by figures which show life expectancy at birth is 71 years for poor children, compared to 82 years for wealthy children [Source 2]. This is a substantial difference of eleven years.

[3 marks – conclusion and information from two sources with evaluative terminology]

The Government's progress towards meeting its targets for 2020.

Conclusion – The Government will make little progress in the next few years.

[1 mark – valid conclusion]

Conclusion – The Government has made little progress toward reducing child poverty in the UK [1 mark valid conclusion]. Source 2 shows us that both relative and absolute poverty will continue to increase.

[2 marks – conclusion and evidence from one source]

Conclusion – The Government will make little progress toward reducing child poverty in the UK [1 mark valid conclusion]. Currently, a quarter of children live in poverty in the UK [Source 1]. Government made a promise to reduce child poverty to 12% for relative poverty by 2020 [Source 1] but Source 3 shows it will actually be 22%.

[3 marks – conclusion and information from two sources]

UK Poverty rates compared to other Countries

Conclusion – UK child poverty rates are higher than most other EU countries

[1 mark valid conclusion]

Conclusion – UK child poverty rates are higher than most other EU countries

[1 mark valid conclusion]

Currently a quarter of children are living in poverty in the UK [Source 1], this is 4% higher than the EU average of 21% [Source 3].

[3 marks – conclusion and evidence from two sources]

Conclusion – UK child poverty rates are among the highest in the EU [1 mark valid conclusion]. Only three EU countries have higher rates of child poverty than the UK, these are Romania, Spain and Italy which are all above the UKs rate of 25% [Source 3]. The UK is also above the EU average of 21% [Source 3].

[3 marks – conclusion and evidence from two sources]

Part D: Crime and the Law

10. *Candidates can be credited in a number of ways* **up to a maximum of 4 marks.**

They can send people to prison.

[1 mark – accurate but undeveloped point]

They can convict criminals and send them to prison. The Sheriff Court can sentence someone for up to five years.

[2 marks – accurate point with development]

They can convict criminals and send them to prison. The Sheriff Court can sentence someone for up to five years. However, if the Sheriff feels this is an insufficient penalty they can refer the case to the High Court where a life sentence is possible.

[3 marks – accurate point with development and exemplification]

Credit reference to aspects of the following:
- Fines
- Community Service
- Community Payback Orders
- Curfews
- ASBOs
- Electronic Tagging

11. *Candidates can be credited in a number of ways **up to a maximum of 8 marks.***

Possible approaches to answering the question:

Drug addiction can cause crime.

[1 mark – accurate but undeveloped point]

Drug addiction can cause crime as addicts need to pay for their drugs and need to steal to fund their habit.

[2 marks – accurate point with development]

Drug addiction can cause crime as addicts need to pay for their drugs and need to steal to fund their habit. Those with drug use dependency are more likely to be arrested for crimes such as burglary, shoplifting or for robbery and handling stolen goods.

[3 marks – accurate point with development and exemplification]

Credit reference to aspects of the following:
- Poverty/deprivation
- Peer pressure
- Family influence
- Alcohol abuse
- Mental Illness
- Violent media images
- Homelessness
- Poor Educational Attainment
- Social Exclusion
- Greed – White collar crime

12. *Candidates can be credited in a number of ways **up to a maximum of 8 marks.***

The level of public awareness of the law concerning social media

Conclusion – A minority of people know about the law.
[1 mark – valid conclusion]

Conclusion – A minority of people know about the law [1 mark – valid conclusion]. This is supported by Source 1 which shows only 1 in 10 know about the law.

[2 marks – conclusion and evidence from one source]

Conclusion – A minority of people know about the law [1 mark – valid conclusion]. This is supported by Source 1 which shows only 1 in 10 know about the law and by Source 2 which tells us 75% of people, a clear majority didn't know about the consequences of being offensive.

[3 marks – conclusion and information from two sources with evaluative terminology]

- More than half of sixteen to eighteen year olds believed it was illegal for an employer to check social media [Source 1].

Social media and the workplace

Conclusion – Employees now have more. rules to follow about the use of social media.

[1 mark – valid conclusion]

Conclusion – Employees now have more rules to follow about the use of social media. [1 mark – valid conclusion] The Gleninch Council have issued a memo to its employees on the appropriate use of social media during work-time [Source 2].

[2 marks – conclusion and evidence from one source]

Conclusion – A lot of working time is being lost due to the use of social media. [1 mark – valid conclusion] The Gleninch Council have issued a memo to its employees on the appropriate use of social media during work-time [Source 2]. This is obviously a problem judging by the increase in the number of hours lost through social media breaks from half an hour to two hours per day [Source 3].

[3 marks – conclusion and information from two sources]
- Social Media breaks are costing more than smoking breaks [Source 3].
- Social Media breaks have quadrupled since 2010 [Source 2].
- Companies now use Social Media to vet applicants [Source 1].
- The Gleninch Council may sack people for inappropriate use of Social Media [Source 2].

Crime associated with social media

Conclusion – There has been an increase in prosecutions relating to social media.

[1 mark – valid conclusion]

Conclusion – There has been an increase in prosecutions relating to social media [1 mark – valid conclusion]. Source 3 shows a huge increase in successful prosecutions.

[2 marks – conclusion and evidence from one source]

Conclusion – Crime related to social media appears to have increased in recent years [1 mark – valid conclusion]. Source 2 shows an increase in the number of incidents reported to the police from 2347 to 2703. However, police have said that many of these (two thirds) are petty online arguments [Source 1].

[3 marks – conclusion and information from two sources]

- More and more people are being prosecuted for their online activities [Source 1].
- Both the number of complaints to the police and of successful prosecutions have increased [Source 2].

Section 3

Part E: World Powers

13. *Candidates can be credited in a number of ways **up to a maximum of 6 marks.***

Possible approaches to answering the question:

CHINA
Other countries rely on China for trade.

[1 mark – accurate but undeveloped point]

North Korea relies on China for both military aid and for food supplies to feed its population.

[2 marks – accurate point with exemplification]

China now manufactures more goods than any other country in the world eg 70% of the world's toys and 50% of the world's clothes. Consumers in places like the USA and the EU rely on China for cheap goods.

[3 marks – accurate point with development and exemplification]

RUSSIA

Other countries rely on Russia for gas supply.

[1 mark – accurate but undeveloped point]

Russia has political influence in the UN. This is because it has a permanent place in the UNSC.

[2 marks – accurate point with exemplification]

The government of Ukraine wanted to build closer economic ties with Western Europe. The recent unrest in Ukraine was a result of conflict between some of their people, who want to stay close to Russia, and their government. Russia has used its military power to arm some Ukrainians which has encouraged a civil war in the eastern parts of the country.

[3 marks – accurate point with development and exemplification]

USA

Other countries rely on the USA for military support.

[1 mark – accurate but undeveloped point]

The US Dollar is like an international currency. Oil is sold in dollars per barrel.

[2 marks – accurate point with exemplification]

The United States has a 'special relationship' with the United Kingdom, a phrase used to describe the close political and economic relations between both countries. Britain has been the USA's strongest supporter in the War on Terror eg bombing IS in Iraq and Syria.

[3 marks – accurate point with development and exemplification]

Credit reference to aspects of the following:
- Trade
- Culture
- Defence
- Diplomatic support
- Ideology
- Environment
- Economic migration
- Finance/Banking
- International Organisations

14. *Candidates can be credited in a number of ways **up to a maximum of 6 marks**.*

Possible approaches to answering the question:

CHINA

Some people are poorly represented in government as they are not in the Communist Party.

[1 mark – accurate point with no development]

Those living and working in rural areas are poorly represented in national government as they are less likely to be members of the Communist Party. The rural Chinese can take part in local committees but these tend to only focus on local issues and not on provincial, national or international issues.

[3 marks – accurate point with development and exemplification]

Credit reference to the following:
- Income/poverty
- Urban/rural divide

- Gender – national government still dominated by men
- Party membership is limited and has restrictions
- Migrant workers may not be registered and cannot participate
- Those with anti-communist views or those who support democratic reform are not well represented and are often silenced by the authorities
- Pressure group activists are not represented especially if they oppose the Communist system

USA

Black Americans are not well represented as there are few Black role models in government.

[1 mark – accurate but undeveloped point]

Black Americans are not well represented as they are more likely to be poor. This tends to mean that they are less likely to run for office.

[2 marks – accurate point with development]

Hispanic Americans are less likely to be represented in government as there is a much lower participation rate among Hispanics. Some have difficulty as English is not their first language so politics and government is difficult for them to understand. This leads to fewer Latinos being elected to high office such as Governor or Senator.

[3 marks – accurate point with development and exemplification]

Credit reference to the following:
- Low paid unskilled work/white collar jobs. Difference in participation leads to difference in representation.
- Blacks and Hispanics experience social and economic inequality as a result of poverty. Apathetic, no role models, other priorities.
- Women remain underrepresented as they either do not run for office or are not chosen by the big two parties, despite the fact that women are more likely to vote in presidential elections.
- Poorly educated are poorly represented and are less likely to vote.
- Some recent immigrants may not have legal status and may lack representation as a result.
- Homeless people may be unlikely to vote and lack representation.

15. *Candidates can be credited in a number of ways **up to a maximum of 8 marks**.*

Possible approaches to answering the question:

Evidence to support the view of Kristen Nunez

In the USA levels of crime have fallen sharply.

[1 mark – accurate use of Source 1 but minimal development]

In the USA levels of crime have fallen sharply. A study from Harvard University says there is no evidence which proves widespread gun ownership among the general population leads to higher incidents of murder.

[2 marks – accurate use of information from different parts of Source 1]

In the USA levels of crime have fallen sharply. A study from Harvard University says there is no evidence which proves widespread gun ownership among the general population leads to higher incidents of murder. This is backed by Source 2 which shows that France has comparatively few gun deaths and they allow gun ownership.

[3 marks – accurate use of information from Sources 1 and 2]

Credit reference to aspects of the following:
- France allows gun ownership but has the second lowest murder rate [Source 3].
- France allows gun ownership but has approximately one third of the violent crime that Russia has [Source 3].
- USA has the highest gun ownership rate but has less than half the murder rate that Russia has [Source 3].

Evidence to oppose the view of Kirsten Nunez

In Source 1 The Brady Campaign to Prevent Gun Violence found that the US firearm homicide rate is 20 times higher than the combined rates of 22 countries with similar levels of wealth.
[1 mark – accurate use of Source 1 but minimal development]

Kristen is wrong as Japan is clearly the safest country as it has by far the lowest murder rate and it does not allow guns of any kind.
[2 marks – accurate use of information from two different Sources]

Credit reference to aspects of the following:
- USA allows gun ownership but has the highest rates of robbery [Source 3].
- Brazil allows guns but has the second highest rate of violent crime and the highest murder rate [Source 3]. Also from Source 2 it has the highest gun deaths.

Part F: World Issues

16. *Candidates can be credited in a number of ways **up to a maximum of 6 marks**.*

African people living in poverty often go hungry.
[1 mark – accurate but undeveloped point]

During a conflict many people have become refugees as their homes have been destroyed by armed forces.
[2 marks – accurate point with development]

Many children in countries like Botswana have been left orphaned by AIDS. This has denied them an education and resulted in a lifetime of poverty. Their health will also be affected as they will be unable to afford health care.
[3 marks – accurate point with development and exemplification]

Credit reference to aspects of the following:
- Poverty
- Ill-health
- Crime/violent assault/murder/rape
- Child soldiers/child labour/child abduction
- Loss of family
- Homeless
- Terrorism
- Piracy
- Nuclear Weapons
- Refugees
- Loss of liberty/kidnapping
- Loss of property/business/job

No marks should be awarded for the identification of the world issue or problem.

17. *Candidates can be credited in a number of ways **up to a maximum of 8 marks**.*

Possible approaches to answering the question:

The conflict in Ukraine has not been solved by the EU as Russia is providing arms to the rebels.
[1 mark – accurate but undeveloped point]

The UN has tried to stop the recent Israel/Palestine conflict by arranging peace talks. It failed as Israel was determined to stop rockets being fired at its territory and ignored the invitation to the peace talks.
[2 marks – accurate point with development]

Piracy is a big problem off the coast of Somalia. The NATO naval task force has been successful as it has around 25 warships which patrol the area and protect shipping. NATO ships have reduced the problem but the area involved is so large and the Somali's are so poor it is probably impossible to stop it totally.
[4 marks – accurate point with development, exemplification and analysis]

Credit reference to aspects of the following
- Libya – success as NATO military power was too much for Libya.
- Libya – failure as tribal/religious rivalries making progress difficult.
- Syria – failure of the UN to agree collective action – Russian veto.
- Syria – the UN have been successful in feeding refugees as they are in neighbouring countries which have offered assistance and are easier to reach.
- Terrorism – success as vast resources committed by NATO.
- Terrorism – failure – religious/ethnic/political feelings are too strong and cannot be easily controlled. Extremists are willing to give their own lives, which is difficult to combat.
- Child Soldiers – War Child has been successful in the Democratic Republic of Congo in that they have accommodated, rehabilitated and reintegrated children who have been displaced from their homes due to conflict.
- Child Soldiers – failure – much of the DR Congo is still desperately poor and still in conflict.

No marks should be awarded for the identification of the world issue or conflict.

18. *Candidates can be credited in a number of ways **up to a maximum of 8 marks**.*

Possible approaches to answering the question:

Evidence to support the view of Ted King

Two aid workers were shot dead in Afghanistan.
[1 mark – accurate source of Source 1 but minimal development]

Afghanistan is a drug producer and it is more dangerous because two aid workers were shot dead in Afghanistan while the murder rate in the USA (a drug using country) has halved.
[2 marks – accurate use of information from different parts of Source 1]

Afghanistan is a drug producer and it is more dangerous because two aid workers were shot dead. Afghanistan also has the second highest number of violent kidnappings. This figure is three times higher than for the highest drug using country, the USA.
[3 marks – accurate use of information from Sources 1 and 3 with evaluative comment]

Credit reference to aspects of the following:
- Colombia has "no-go" areas (Source 1).
- Colombia has highest murder rate (Source 3).
- Colombia has highest kidnapping rate (Source 3).
- All three producers have very high kidnappings (Source 3).

- El Salvador (user) has reduced its murder rate by 80% (Source 1).
- USA (user) murder rate has fallen (Source 1).

Evidence to oppose the view of Ted King

The USA is more dangerous as it has the most drug related crime at 104 per 100,000. This is nearly double the highest drug producing country, Colombia.

[2 marks – accurate use of Source 2 with evaluative comment]

Ted is wrong as the USA is more dangerous. One gang member admitted killing forty people and it has far more serious assaults at 874.

[2 marks – accurate use of information from two different Sources]

Ted is clearly wrong as the USA (not a drug producer) is more dangerous. One gang member admitted killing forty people and it has far more serious assaults than any of the drug producers at 874. The highest figure in the drug producing countries is 100 in Peru which is only around a ninth of the USA figure.

[3 marks – accurate use of information from two sources with evaluative comment]

Credit reference to aspects of the following:
- President says Afghanistan is safer (Source 1).
- Lowest total crime rates are in Colombia and Peru (Source 2).
- USA has highest total crime rate (Source 2).
- USA has most drug crime (Source 2).
- Afghanistan has the lowest murder rate (Source 3).
- USA has the most serious assaults (Source 3).

NATIONAL 5 MODERN STUDIES 2017

Part A: Democracy in Scotland

1. *Candidates can be credited in a number of ways* **up to a maximum of 4 marks.**

   Possible approaches to answering the question:

   People in Scotland have the right to vote in elections.

   [1 mark – accurate but undeveloped point]

   People in Scotland have the right to vote in elections such as the Scottish Parliament elections.

   [2 marks – accurate with development]

   People in Scotland have the right to vote in elections such as the Scottish Parliament elections. For example, the last Scottish Parliament election was held in May 2016 when the SNP won 63 seats, allowing them to form the government.

   [3 marks – accurate point with development and exemplification]]

   Credit reference to aspects of the following:
   - Right to free speech
   - Right to protest
   - Right to join a group (pressure group, trade union or political party)
   - Right to lobby a representative
   - Right to organise/sign a petition.

2. *Candidates can be credited in a number of ways* **up to a maximum of 8 marks.**

   Some political parties' election campaigns are successful because of their use of social media.

   [1 mark – accurate but undeveloped]

   Some political parties' election campaigns are successful because of their use of social media. This allows them to reach a large number of voters and tell them about their policies.

   [2 marks – accurate with development]

   Some political parties' election campaigns are successful because of their use of social media. This allows them to reach a large number of voters and tell them about their policies. Most political parties now have Facebook and Twitter pages. For example, the SNP has over 150,000 followers on Twitter.

   [4 marks – accurate with development and exemplification]

   Credit reference to aspects of the following:
   - Party membership
   - Party funding
   - Use of other media, eg television, radio
   - Support of the printed press
   - Party image
   - Party leader
   - Constituency party activists.

   Credit reference to aspects of unsuccessful political parties' election campaigns, where appropriate.

3. *Candidates can be credited in a number of ways* **up to a maximum of 8 marks.**

   Possible approaches to answering the question:

   Public support in North Clydeburgh for Savings Proposal 3

Conclusion – There is support for Savings Proposal 3 in North Clydeburgh.
[1 mark – valid conclusion]

Conclusion – People in North Clydeburgh support Savings Proposal 3. For example, in a survey of public opinion on North Clydeburgh's savings proposals 60% said yes (source 2).
[2 marks – conclusion and evidence from one source]

Conclusion – Savings Proposal 3 would be the most popular option for people in North Clydeburgh. Savings Proposal 3 is for the council to reduce refuse collection along the beach areas (source 3). The public opinion survey on North Clydeburgh Council's saving proposals show that a majority of people in North Clydeburgh, 60%, said they supported reducing refuse collection at local beaches, all of the other options only had support of 30% or less (source 2).
[3 marks – conclusion and information from two sources with evaluative terminology]

The impact on council services of Savings Proposal 2

Conclusion – Savings Proposal 2 will mean the council can't improve the care services for the elderly.
[1 mark – valid conclusion]

Conclusion – Savings Proposal 2 will mean the council can't improve the care services for the elderly. For example, spending on elderly services will be reduced by £20 million (source 3).
[2 marks – conclusion and evidence from one source]

Conclusion – Savings Proposal 2 will mean North Clydeburgh Council will be unable to improve the care services for the elderly. Savings Proposal 2 wants to reduce spending on care for the elderly by £20 million (source 3) however the leader of North Clydeburgh Council recently said they have to spend more money on services for the elderly, according to the leader an extra £10 million was needed to be spent on improving elderly care (source 1). Savings proposal 2 will mean they will not have enough money to make the improvements.
[3 marks – conclusion and information from **two** sources]

How successfully will North Clydeburgh Council's Savings proposals achieve their savings target

Conclusion – North Clydeburgh Council's saving proposals will not achieve their savings target.
[1 mark – valid conclusion]

Conclusion – North Clydeburgh Council's saving proposals will not achieve their savings target. The proposals will only save the council £70 million (source 3).
[2 marks – conclusion and evidence from one source]

Conclusion – North Clydeburgh Council's saving proposals will not achieve their savings target. North Clydeburgh Council has a savings target of £75 million (source 1) however the chart shows that the savings from all of the proposals will only achieve a saving of £70 million (source 3). This is £5 million less than their overall target and this means their target will not be met.
[3 marks – conclusion and information from **two** sources with evaluative terminology]

Any other valid reason that meets the criteria described in the general marking instructions for this kind of question.

Part B: Democracy in the United Kingdom

4. *Candidates can be credited in a number of ways **up to a maximum of 4 marks**.*

Possible approaches to answering the question:

People in the UK have the right to vote in elections.
[1 mark – accurate but undeveloped point]

People in the UK have the right to vote in elections such as the General Election.
[2 marks – accurate with development]

People in the UK have the right to vote in elections such as the General Election. For example, the last General Election was held in May 2015 when the Conservative Party won 331 seats in the House of Commons, allowing them to form the government.
[3 marks – accurate point with development and exemplification]

Credit reference to aspects of the following:
- Right to free speech
- Right to protest
- Right to join a group (pressure group, trade union or political party)
- Right to lobby a representative
- Right to organise/sign a petition.

Any other valid point that meets the criteria described in the general marking instructions for this kind of question.

5. *Candidates can be credited in a number of ways **up to a maximum of 8 marks**.*

Some political parties' election campaigns are successful because of their use of social media.
[1 mark – accurate but undeveloped]

Some political parties' election campaigns are successful because of their use of social media. This allows them to reach a large number of voters and tell them about their policies.
[2 marks – accurate with development]

Some political parties' election campaigns are successful because of their use of social media. This allows them to reach a large number of voters and tell them about their policies. Most political parties now have Facebook and Twitter pages. For example, the Conservatives have over 220,000 followers on Twitter.
[4 marks – accurate with development and exemplification]

Credit reference to aspects of the following:
- Party membership
- Party funding
- Use of other media, eg television, radio
- Support of the printed press
- Party image
- Party leader
- Constituency party activists.

Any other valid point that meets the criteria described in the general marking instructions for this kind of question.

6. *Candidates can be credited in a number of ways **up to a maximum of 8 marks**.*

Possible approaches to answering the question:

The UK electoral performance of the Conservative Party compared to 2010

Conclusion – The Conservative Party performed better in the 2015 General Election than 2010.
[1 mark – valid conclusion]

Conclusion – The Conservative Party performed better in the 2015 General Election than 2010. In source 1 it states that the exit polls correctly predicted they would be the biggest single party in the House of Commons.

[2 marks – valid conclusion and evidence from one source]

Conclusion – The Conservative Party performed better in the 2015 General Election than 2010. In source 1 it stated that the exit polls correctly predicted they would be the biggest single party in the House of Commons. This can be linked to source 2 which tells us the Conservative gained the share of the UK vote, 37% which was an increase from 2010.

[3 marks – valid conclusion and evidence from two sources]

The UK electoral performance of the Liberal Democrats compared to 2010

Conclusion – The Liberal Democrats performed very poorly in 2015 compared to their 2010 result.

[1 mark – valid conclusion]

Conclusion – The Liberal Democrats performed very poorly in 2015 compared to their 2010 result. In source 1 it states that the Liberal Democrats saw a significant drop in both their UK share of the vote and in the number of MPs returned to the House of Commons.

[2 marks – valid conclusion and evidence from one source]

Conclusion – The Liberal Democrats performed very poorly in 2015 compared to their 2010 result. In source 1 it states that the Liberal Democrats saw a significant drop in both their UK share of the vote and in the number of MPs returned to the House of Commons. This can be supported by source 2 that shows that the seats won by the Liberal Democrats fell by 49, which means they only managed to get 8 MPs elected compared to their 57 MPs in 2010.

[3 marks – valid conclusion and evidence from two sources]

The dominant political party in Scotland after the General Election

Conclusion – The Scottish National Party (SNP) was the dominant political party in Scotland after the 2015 general election.

[1 mark – valid conclusion]

Conclusion – The Scottish National Party (SNP) was the dominant political party in Scotland after the 2015 General Election. In source 1 it states that Labour was crushed by the Scottish National Party under the leadership of Nicola Sturgeon with 56 MPs elected to the House of Commons.

[2 marks – valid conclusion and evidence from one source]

Conclusion – The Scottish National Party (SNP) was the dominant political party in Scotland after the 2015 General Election. In source 1 it states that Labour was crushed by the Scottish National Party under the leadership of Nicola Sturgeon with 56 MPs elected to the House of Commons. This can be linked to source 3 that clearly shows that the SNP won 50% of the vote in Scotland which was an increase of 30% since the 2010 general election.

[3 marks – valid conclusion and evidence from two sources]

Any other valid reason that meets the criteria described in the general marking instructions for this kind of question.

Part C: Social Inequality

7. *Candidates can be credited in a number of ways up to a maximum of 6 marks.*

Possible approaches to answering the question:

One consequence of social inequalities on communities is that businesses may leave the area.

[1 mark – accurate but undeveloped]

One consequence of social inequalities on communities is that businesses may leave the area. This means that people living in the area have less access to certain services.

[2 marks – accurate and developed]

One consequence of social inequalities on communities is that businesses may leave the area. This means that people living in the area have less access to certain services and have to travel further to meet their needs. For example, people may have to spend money in order to travel to large retail parks to access a supermarket.

[3 marks – accurate with development and exemplification]

Credit reference to aspects of the following:
- Lower educational attainment
- Higher crime rates eg vandalism and anti-social behaviour
- Unemployment
- House prices
- Social exclusion.

Any other valid point that meets the criteria described in the general marking instructions for this kind of question.

8. *Candidates can be credited in a number of ways up to a maximum of 6 marks.*

Possible approaches to answering the question:

One reason why people are more likely to suffer social inequalities is discrimination.

[1 mark – accurate but undeveloped]

One reason why people are more likely to suffer social inequalities is discrimination. Women are often paid less than men even when they do the same job.

[2 marks accurate and developed]

One reason why people are more likely to suffer social inequalities is discrimination. Women are often paid less than men even when they do the same job. For example, in the UK, the pay-gap is approximately 19%.

[3 marks accurate with development and exemplification]

Credit reference to aspects of the following:
- Other forms of discrimination, eg ageism, racism
- Unemployment
- Lone parents
- Low income
- Geographical location
- Poverty cycle.

Any other relevant factual key point of knowledge that meets the criteria described in the general marking instructions for this kind of question.

9. *Candidates can be credited in a number of ways up to a maximum of 8 marks.*

Possible approaches to answering the question:

Supporting the view 'Foodbanks are an effective solution to food poverty.'

Foodbanks have fed over 1 million people who would have been hungry without this essential service.

[1 mark – evidence drawn from source 1]

Foodbanks help to prevent crime, housing loss, family breakdown and mental health problems (source 1). Local police have issued food vouchers to prevent shoplifting (source 3).

[2 marks – evidence linked from source 1 and source 3]

Source 1 shows there has been a huge rise from 346,992 to over 1 million people using foodbanks which shows that they are needed. This can be linked to the 15% rise in the cost of food shown in source 2 and the rise in the numbers of children and working age adults without children who live in absolute poverty.

[3 marks – evidence linked from source 1 and 2 with evaluative terminology]

Credit reference to aspects of the following:
- Foodbanks also make time to chat and direct clients to other helpful services such as debt advice and career guidance (source 1)
- Large increases in household bills eg gas and electricity mean people have less money to spend on food (source 2)
- There has been a doubling in food poverty over the last four years (source 1).

Opposing the view 'Foodbanks are an effective solution to food poverty.'

Foodbanks are not an effective solution: the community representative in source 3 points out that they are only on the rise because it's free and because it's there.

[1 mark – evidence drawn from source 3]

Some household bills have actually decreased: broadband bills are 40% less in 2016 than they were in 2013 and rent and council tax have only gone up by a small percentage therefore people should have enough money to spend on food. The number of working age parents living in absolute poverty has not increased much since 2009 and so there is no need for food banks.

[3 marks – evidence linked from within source 2 with evaluative terminology]

Credit reference to aspects of the following:
- A useful emergency stopgap: not a long term solution
- Not really needed: people who spend all their benefits use foodbanks (source 3)
- Foodbanks don't help people with long term issues, such as addiction, alcoholism and mental illness. A local council is spending over £240,000 on foodbanks. It would be better spent on addiction clinics (source 3)
- Must address the real reasons why people can't afford food (source 3)
- Higher wages are a better solution to food poverty (source 3)
- Free school meals are a better solution to food poverty (source 3).

Any other valid reason that meets the criteria described in the general marking instructions for this kind of question.

Part D: Crime and the Law

10. *Candidates can be credited in a number of ways up to a maximum of 6 marks.*

    Possible approaches to answering the question:

    One consequence of crime on communities is that local businesses may leave an area with high crime rates.

    [1 mark – accurate but undeveloped point]

Communities with high crime rates will gain a negative reputation. People may start to stereotype individuals from areas of high crime, leading to social problems and a lack of opportunities in that area. For example, the provision of local services will suffer as businesses will not want to set up in areas with high crime rates, which will limit employment opportunities.

[3 marks – accurate point with development and exemplification]

Credit reference to aspects of the following:
- Consequences of crime on communities
- Areas will become run down, vandalism
- Rise in unemployment rate
- Businesses will leave
- Fear created
- People will move in order to find safety
- Lower house price values
- Lack of successful role models in the area
- Empower local communities – fight against crime.

Any other valid point that meets the criteria described in the general marking instructions for this kind of question.

11. *Candidates can be credited in a number of ways up to a maximum of 6 marks.*

    Possible approaches to answering the question:

    One reason why some people are more likely to commit crime than others is due to peer pressure.

    [1 mark – accurate but undeveloped point]

    One reason that some people are more likely to commit crimes than others is due to peer pressure. Young people can be pressurised into joining gangs and are sometimes forced to take part in initiation tasks.

    [2 marks – accurate and developed]

    One reason that some people are more likely to commit crimes than others is due to peer pressure. Young people can be pressurised into joining gangs and are sometimes forced to take part in initiation tasks. This can lead to other criminal activities associated with gangs such as knife crime, vandalism and anti-social behaviour.

    [3 marks – accurate with development and exemplification]

    Credit reference to aspects of the following:
    - Poverty/deprivation
    - Peer pressure
    - Family influence
    - Alcohol abuse
    - Mental illness
    - Violent media images
    - Homelessness
    - Poor educational attainment
    - Social exclusion
    - Greed – white collar crime.

    Any other relevant factual key point of knowledge that meets the criteria described in the general marking instructions for this kind of question.

12. *Candidates can be credited in a number of ways up to a maximum of 8 marks.*

    Possible approaches to answering the question:

    Samara Ezra is supported (not selective) in her view, "Police Scotland is successfully tackling serious organised crime".

    Candidates should give evidence from the sources that support Samara Ezra's view.

Samara's view is supported (not selective) as source 1 states that Police Scotland has built partnerships with the public to tackle drugs crime and reduce the sale of counterfeit goods. Thousands of counterfeit CDs and DVDs have been seized during an intelligence led operation in Glasgow.

[1 mark – accurate use of source 1 but no development]

Samara's view is supported (not selective) as Police Scotland are cooperating much more with European organisations such as Europol to increase the exchange of intelligence to and from Scotland. This is supported by source 3 which says Police Scotland are also now working closely with HM Revenues and Customs and other European agencies to monitor and share information, in the fight against organised crime.

[2 marks – evidence linked from sources 1 and 3]

Credit reference to aspects of the following:
- Police Scotland has built partnerships with the public to tackle drugs crime and reduce the sale of counterfeit goods. Thousands of counterfeit CDs and DVDs have been seized during an intelligence led operation in Glasgow. This can be demonstrated in the dramatic increase in the amount of drug seizures that have happened between 2013 and 2016. For example, class C drugs have nearly doubled from 3311 to 5463 between 2013 and 2016. (sources 1 and 2)
- Source 3 states that "The Scottish Government however have tried to help by tightening the laws surrounding what people can be prosecuted for in relation to organised crime". This links with source 1 which states that "New offences have been introduced which has led to the conviction of those involved in organised crime." and "Police Scotland has stated that even with these difficulties, they have increased the number of arrests in relation to organised crime." Finally, if you look at source 2 that has been a steady increase between 2013 and 2016 in the number of arrests associated with organised crime. (sources 1, 2 and 3)

Samara Ezra is opposed (selective) in her view, "Police Scotland is successfully tackling serious organised crime."

Candidates should give evidence from the sources that oppose Samara Ezra's view.

Samara Ezra's view is opposed (selective) because it says in source 1, "the Police find it very difficult to investigate and monitor communications. It is currently too easy for the key figures in organised crime to carry out their illegal activities online". This is supported by source 3 which says that "Criminals are now using apps, such as WhatsApp and BBM, which are based on their smart phones to contact each other. This means that they do not have itemised bills and it is much more difficult to trace and investigate them." This is supported further in source 2 where it shows that between 2013 and 2016 the most of the communications that was done in 2013 by people involved in organised crime was telephone calls and this had changed to WhatsApp and BBM in 2016.

[3 marks — accurate information from three sources with some evaluative terminology used regarding the pie charts in source 2, ie "most"]

Credit reference to aspects of the following:
- The budget for Police Scotland needs to be increased from £1.1 billion to £1.3 billion to address the issues that have arisen concerning investigating organised crime. (source 1)

- Police Scotland is hindered by the strict guidelines imposed which limits the types of communication methods they have access to in an investigation. This links with source 1 which states "To improve performance, a government committee needs to be set up in order to investigate how Police Scotland can work with communication companies in their fight against organised crime." (sources 1 and 3)

Any other valid reason that meets the criteria described in the general marking instructions for this kind of question.

Part E: World Powers

13. *Candidates can be credited in a number of ways* **up to a maximum of 4 marks.**

Possible approaches to answering the question:

The world power that I have studied is the USA. One of the causes of socio-economic issues is unemployment.

[1 mark – accurate but undeveloped]

The world power that I have studied is the USA. One of the causes of socio-economic issues is unemployment. This can lead to people living in poverty and struggling to meet their needs.

[2 marks – accurate and developed]

The world power that I have studied is China. One of the causes of socio-economic issues is migration. This can lead to people living in poverty and struggling to meet their needs. For example, migrant workers can struggle to find employment and are unable to support their families.

[3 marks – accurate with development and exemplification]

Credit reference to aspects of the following:
- Low income
- Low education attainment
- Poor health
- Discrimination eg racism
- Illegal immigration
- Government strategies.

Any other valid point that meets the criteria described in the general marking instructions for this kind of question.

14. *Candidates can be credited in a number of ways* **up to a maximum of 6 marks.**

Possible approaches to answering the question:

The world power that I have studied is Brazil. One reason why many people who live in the Favelas are less likely to participate in politics is because of lack of education.

[1 mark – accurate but undeveloped]

The world power that I have studied is Brazil. One reason why many people who live in the Favelas are less likely to participate in politics is because of lack of education. They often do not attend school because they have to work to support their families from a young age.

[2 marks – accurate and developed]

The world power that I have studied is Brazil. One reason why many people who live in the Favelas are less likely to participate in politics is because of lack of education. They often do not attend school because they have to work to support their families from a young age. For example, in the recent government impeachment "coup", many residents of the Favelas stated that their priority was to survive daily life, rather than participate in politics.

[3 marks – accurate with development and exemplification]

Credit reference to aspects of the following:
- Lack of role models
- Language barriers
- Corrupt officials/government leaders
- Discrimination eg gender, ethnicity
- Human rights
- Geographical location eg rural/urban.

Any other relevant factual key point of knowledge that meets the criteria described in the general marking instructions for this kind of question.

15. *Candidates can be credited in a number of ways **up to a maximum of 10 marks**.*

Possible approaches to answering the question:

For Option One: Serbia is allowed to join the European Union

Serbia should be allowed to join the European Union, evidence to support this can be found in source 1 where it states that "Serbia has made significant progress in meeting the Copenhagen Criteria". The Copenhagen Criteria states that countries who wish to join should have "a stable democracy, the rule of law, human rights and respect for and protection of minorities". This is backed up in source 3 where it states that "crime rates in Serbia are at an all-time low."

[3 marks – detailed evidence linked from sources 1 and 3]

Credit reference to aspects of the following:
- The government in Serbia is working well with the European Parliament to ensure all negotiating is running smoothly (source 1)
- Serbia has also recently become a member of the Western Balkan group and is forming relationships in their own region (source 1)
- The EU is currently Serbia's biggest trading and investment partner (source 1)
- 51% of the public in Serbia either agree or strongly agree with Serbia joining the European Union (source 2)
- Serbia-Germany cooperation is important for Serbia on the road to EU membership (source 2)
- Croatia supports EU enlargement to include Serbia, having in the past blocked it (source 2)
- Crime rates in Serbia are at an all-time low. There has been a large scale police crackdown on drugs this year and they arrested 30 drug smugglers in a joint operation with Germany (source 3)
- 3% growth of the Serbian economy in 2016 (source 3).

Reasons for rejecting other option:

Option 2: Serbia should not be allowed to join the European Union

I did not choose option 2 as although some people may say that Serbia have not made a lot of progress, they have recently taken part in EU-led peace talks between Serbia and Kosovo.

[1 mark – awarded for use of one piece of information with no linking. Do not credit if marks have already been awarded for this point]

Serbia should not be allowed to join the European Union as "many people in Serbia feel an alliance with Russia

would be better for their economy rather than joining the EU".

[1 mark – evidence drawn from source 3]

Serbia should not be allowed to join the European Union as they have not made great progress toward meeting the Copenhagen Criteria, they have still not met the following criteria discussed in source 1, "a stable economy and low unemployment" as it states in source 3 that "floods in Serbia in 2014, had a negative impact on their economy".

[2 marks – evidence linked from sources 1 and 3]

Credit reference to aspects of the following:
- The European Council has however postponed negotiations with Serbia on two chapters of EU legislation after a complaint from the Croatian government, demanding better treatment of Croats in Serbia and more action on war crimes (source 1)
- Human rights are still not as protected as they should be, with freedom of the media still a concern. In early July, a newspaper editor was severely beaten by three men who demanded money and were not happy about the newspaper's political views (source 1)
- Uncertainty for countries wishing to join the EU due to Brexit (source 2)
- Greece, Bulgaria and Serbia meet to discuss the migrant crisis (source 2)
- Migrants fleeing Syria are putting pressure on lots of members of the EU, this is causing conflict between members (source 3)
- Many countries in the EU are getting worried about enlargement and don't want other countries to join (source 3)

Reasons for rejecting the other option:

Although many people would argue that Serbia has made great progress in meeting their targets, Serbia should not be allowed to join the European Union as in source 3 it states that many people in Serbia "feel an alliance with Russia would be better for their economy rather than joining the EU". This is backed up in source 2 where the graph shows that 50% of the people in the opinion poll either agreed or strongly agreed that Serbia would be better off in an alliance with Russia rather than in the EU. This shows that lots of people do in fact think that Russia would be a better economic alliance that the EU.

[3 marks – evidence drawn from two sources, with evaluative comment]

Any other valid reason that meets the criteria described in the general marking instructions for this kind of question.

Part F: World Issues

16. *Candidates can be credited in a number of ways **up to a maximum of 4 marks**.*

Possible approaches to answering the question:

The civil war in Syria has led to many refugees.

[1 mark – accurate but undeveloped point]

The civil war in Syria has led to many refugees and forced people to leave their homes and go to countries such as Lebanon.

[2 marks – accurate with exemplification]

The civil war in Syria has led to many refugees and forced people to leave their homes and go to countries such as Lebanon. People left the city of Homs as the

Syrian army and opposition fighters were fighting for control of the city and over 16,000 people died.

[3 marks – accurate point with development and detailed exemplification]

Credit reference to aspects of the following:
• Migration
• Piracy
• Terrorism
• Child soldiers
• Poverty
• Hunger
• Climate change.

Any other valid point that meets the criteria described in the general marking instructions for this kind of question.

17. *Candidates can be credited in a number of ways **up to a maximum of 6 marks**.*

Possible approaches to answering the question:

The United Nations has provided aid to Sierra Leone to stop ebola spreading further.

[1 mark – accurate but undeveloped point]

The United Nations has provided aid to Sierra Leone to stop ebola spreading further. UN agencies such as WHO have sent medical staff to train local healthcare workers so that they have the skills to be self-sufficient.

[2 marks – accurate with development]

The United Nations has provided aid to Sierra Leone to stop ebola spreading further. UN agencies such as WHO have sent medical staff to train local healthcare workers so that they have the skills to be self-sufficient. WHO has also worked in partnership with developed countries such as the UK to build local treatment centres to care for those affected.

[3 marks – accurate point with development and exemplification]

Credit reference to aspects of the following:
• UN
• African Union
  – Common borders mean conflicts can have a direct impact eg in Zimbabwe and Kenya
  – AU has a Child's Charter and so must work to prevent child soldiers, exploitation
• NATO
  – Charter sets out collective responsibilities
  Crisis management one of its aims; political, military or humanitarian
• EU
  – impact on member states eg migration, refugees, nearby conflicts such as Syria and Georgia
• NGO
  – Purpose is to work in specific field eg Oxfam in famine hit areas.

Any other relevant factual key point of knowledge that meets the criteria described in the general marking instructions for this kind of question.

18. *Candidates can be credited in a number of ways **up to a maximum of 10 marks**.*

Possible approaches to answering the question:

For Option 1:

I would choose option 1 because source 1 states 43% of the population of country Y live below the poverty line. This is supported in source 2 when 55% of people surveyed said the government should increase the minimum wage.

[2 marks – evidence linked from sources 1 and 2]

I would choose option 1 because source 1 states 43% of the population of country Y live below the poverty line. This is supported in source 2 when 55% of people surveyed said the government should increase the minimum wage. This highlights that there are huge numbers of people living in poverty and more than half of the people surveyed support option 1.

[3 marks – evidence linked from sources 1 and 2 with evaluation]

Credit reference to aspects of the following:
• More than 3 million people requiring food aid (source 1)
• Housing costs are extremely high in relation to wages (source 1)
• Many workers have little money left after housing costs (source 3)
• Low wages restrict access to medical treatment (source 3).

Reason for rejecting other option:

I could have chosen option 2 because in source 1 it states previous increases in minimum hourly wages have been viewed negatively by businesses, however, I picked option 1 because in source 3, it states many workers have little money left after housing costs.

[2 marks – evidence linked between two sources]

For Option 2:

I would choose option 2 because source 1 states that many people think that the high unemployment rate is a direct result of previous increases in the hourly minimum wage. This is supported in source 2 where the opinion poll highlights 60% either agree or strongly agree that the government should introduce income support rather than minimum wage.

[2 marks – evidence linked from sources 1 and 2]

I would choose option 2 because source 1 states that many people think that the high unemployment rate is a direct result of previous increases in the hourly minimum wage. This is supported in source 2 where the opinion poll highlights 60% either agree or strongly agree that the government should introduce income support rather than minimum wage. This highlights that the majority of people are against the minimum wage.

[3 marks – evidence linked from sources 1 and 2 with evaluation]

Credit reference to aspects of the following:
• The President of country Y stated an increase in pay should not be related to the cost of living but should be linked to productivity (source 1)
• Increases in minimum wage are viewed negatively by businesses as well as agricultural workers (source 1)
• Recent increases in minimum wage have a major impact on businesses (source 3)
• A further increase will result in greater unemployment (source 3).

Reasons for rejecting the other option:

I could have chosen option 1 because in source 3 it states many workers have little money left after housing costs, however, I picked option 2 because it states in source 1, previous increases in minimum hourly wages have been viewed negatively by businesses.

[2 marks – evidence linked between **two** sources]

Any other valid reason that meets the criteria described in the general marking instructions for this kind of question.

NATIONAL 5 MODERN STUDIES
2017 SPECIMEN QUESTION PAPER

Part A: Democracy in Scotland

1. *Candidates can be credited in a number of ways **up to a maximum of 4 marks**.*

Possible approaches to answering the question:

Political parties can campaign during a Scottish Parliament election by canvassing.
[1 mark – accurate but undeveloped point]

Political parties can campaign during a Scottish Parliament election by canvassing. Canvassing gives parties the opportunity to go door to door to speak with the public in an attempt to increase voter awareness of the party.
[2 marks – developed point]

Political parties can campaign during a Scottish Parliament election by canvassing. Canvassing gives parties the opportunity to go door to door to speak with the public in an attempt to increase voter awareness of the party. This may secure more votes for the party as the canvassers will outline and explain the party policies to be implemented once elected.
[3 marks – developed point with detail and exemplification]

Credit reference to aspects of the following:
- Use of the media – newspapers, PEBs, TV debates, social media
- Leafleting
- Posters
- Holding a public meeting/rally
- Publishing a manifesto
- Use of celebrities to gain media attention and support from voters.

Any other valid point that meets the criteria described in the general marking instructions.

2. *Candidates can be credited in a number of ways **up to a maximum of 6 marks**.*

Possible approaches to answering the question:

The Scottish Parliament has responsibility for devolved matters such as education.
[1 mark – accurate but undeveloped point]

The Scottish Parliament has responsibility for devolved matters such as education. Scottish pupils sit Nationals and Highers whereas English students sit GCSEs, AS and A-Levels.
[2 marks – developed point]

The Scottish Parliament has responsibility for devolved matters such as education. Scottish pupils sit Nationals and Highers whereas English students sit GCSEs, AS and A-Levels. In 2017 the Scottish Government introduced the revised National 5 to be examined for the first time in 2018.
[3 marks – developed point with exemplification]

Credit reference to aspects of the following:
- Health
- Local government
- Law, including most aspects of criminal and civil law, the prosecution system and the courts
- Social work
- Housing
- Tourism and economic development.

Any other valid point that meets the criteria described in the general marking instructions.

3. (a) *Candidates can be credited in a number of ways **up to a maximum of 8 marks**.*

Possible approaches to answering the question:

The Additional Member System is a more proportional system.
[1 mark – accurate but undeveloped point]

The Additional Member System is a more proportional system because the percentage of votes relates to the percentage of seats won by a party.
[2 marks – developed point]

The Additional Member System is a more proportional system because the percentage of votes relates to the percentage of seats won by a party. For example, in the 2011 election the Conservatives won about 12% of the vote and 12% of the seats.
[3 marks – developed point with exemplification]

The Additional Member System is a broadly proportional system because the percentage of votes relates to the percentage of seats won by a party. For example, in the 2011 election the Conservatives won about 12% of the vote and 12% of the seats. This can often lead to coalition governments, as no one party has a majority, which means parties work together providing better representation for voters.
[4 marks – developed point with exemplification and analysis]

Credit reference to aspects of the following:
- Retains elements of FPTP so some direct representation – voters in every constituency know who to contact
- Greater choice – each voter can contact a number of MSPs due to the regional list element
- Greater choice – two votes at the ballot box
- Smaller parties can be successful, eg Greens in Scottish Parliament.

Any other valid point that meets the criteria described in the general marking instructions.

(b) *Candidates can be credited in a number of ways **up to a maximum of 8 marks**.*

Possible approaches to answering the question:

Trade Unions

People may join a trade union to protect their rights at work.
[1 mark – accurate but undeveloped point]

People may join a trade union to protect their rights at work. For example, most secondary teachers join the EIS or SSTA.
[2 marks – accurate with exemplification]

People may join a trade union to protect their rights at work. For example, most teachers join the EIS or SSTA. They might do this because they feel that they are being asked to complete work out with their job description. The trade union will take action on their behalf eg trade unions have had discussions with the Scottish Government over unit assessments in secondary school.
[4 marks – accurate point with development and detailed exemplification]

Credit reference to aspects of the following:

Trade Unions
- Protect rights at work eg health and safety, pay, holidays, pensions
- TUs have experience negotiating with management
- TUs have legal teams you can use
- Collective action is more effective than individual action.

Pressure Groups

People may choose to join a pressure group because they are passionate about a cause.

[1 mark – accurate but undeveloped point]

People may choose to join a pressure group because they are passionate about a cause. They may choose to join Greenpeace if they are concerned about the environment.

[2 marks – developed point]

People may choose to join a pressure group because they are passionate about a cause. They may choose to join Greenpeace if they are concerned about the environment. They feel that by joining a pressure group they can have more of an impact by campaigning with other people. For example, Greenpeace has 11,000 Scottish members; this gives it strength in numbers and increases its chances of influencing the government.

[4 marks – accurate point with developed exemplification and analysis]

Credit reference to aspects of the following:

Pressure Groups
- Believe strongly about an issue such as human rights
- Collective action more effective than individual
- Media pay more attention to organised pressure groups
- Pressure groups have experience of campaigning/ protesting
- Seen as the best way to influence government in between elections.

Any other valid point that meets the criteria described in the general marking instructions.

Part B: Democracy in the United Kingdom

4. *Candidates can be credited in a number of ways up to a maximum of 4 marks.*

Possible approaches to answering the question:

Political parties can campaign during a General Election by canvassing.

[1 mark – accurate but undeveloped point]

Political parties can campaign during a General Election by canvassing. Canvassing gives parties the opportunity to go door to door to speak with the public in an attempt to increase voter awareness of the party.

[2 marks – developed point]

Political parties can campaign during a General Election by canvassing. Canvassing gives parties the opportunity to go door to door to speak with the public in an attempt to increase voter awareness of the party. This may secure more votes for the party as the canvassers will outline and explain the party policies to be implemented once elected.

[3 marks – developed point with detail and exemplification]

Credit reference to aspects of the following:
- Use of the media – newspapers, PEBS, TV debates, social media
- Leafleting
- Posters
- Holding a public meeting/rally
- Publishing a manifesto
- Use of celebrities to gain media attention and support from voters.

Any other valid point that meets the criteria described in the general marking instructions.

5. *Candidates can be credited in a number of ways up to a maximum of 6 marks.*

Possible approaches to answering the question:

The UK Parliament has responsibility for reserved matters such as immigration.

[1 mark – accurate but undeveloped point]

The UK Parliament has responsibility for reserved matters such as immigration. Every year they make a number of decisions about who has the right to visit or stay in the country.

[2 marks – developed point]

The UK Parliament has responsibility for reserved matters such as immigration. Every year they make a number of decisions about who has the right to visit or stay in the country. The UK Parliament does, however, work with the Scottish Parliament on this matter in relation to asylum seekers who are living in Scotland.

[3 marks – developed point with exemplification]

Credit reference to aspects of the following:
- Immigration
- Benefits & social security
- Defence
- Foreign policy
- Nuclear power.

Any other valid point that meets the criteria described in the general marking instructions.

6. (a) *Candidates can be credited in a number of ways up to a maximum of 8 marks.*

Possible approaches to answering the question:

One disadvantage of FPTP is that small parties are underrepresented.

[1 mark – accurate but undeveloped point]

One disadvantage of FPTP is that small parties are underrepresented. This is because the percentage of seats which a party wins in Parliament does not represent the percentage of votes they win in the election.

[2 marks – developed point]

One disadvantage of FPTP is that small parties are underrepresented. This is because the percentage of seats which a party wins in Parliament does not represent the percentage of votes they win in the election. In the 2015 General Election, UKIP got 12.6% of the votes (almost four million votes) and 1 seat.

[3 marks – developed point with exemplification]

One disadvantage of FPTP is that small parties are underrepresented because the percentage of seats which a party wins in Parliament does not represent the percentage of votes they win in the election. In the 2015 General Election, UKIP got 12.6% of the votes (almost four million votes) and 1 seat. This is unfair and is a reason why some people believe that FPTP is undemocratic and, as a result, do not vote.

[4 marks – developed point with exemplification and analysis]

Credit reference to aspects of the following:
- If party support is spread out and not concentrated in a constituency, parties
- Will find it very difficult to get any MPs elected
- Tactical voting is possible
- There are no prizes for second place
- In safe seats parties have a great power to choose the MP
- Many won't vote for smaller parties in a safe seat

- Strong government isn't always good government
- Political parties often target marginal seats and can be seen to ignore constituencies with safe seats.

Any valid point that meets the criteria described in the general marking instructions.

(b) *Candidates can be credited in a number of ways up to a maximum of 8 marks.*

Possible approaches to answering the question:

Trade Unions

People may join a trade union to protect their rights at work.
[1 mark – accurate but undeveloped point]

People may join a trade union to protect their rights at work. For example, rail workers join the Rail, Maritime and Transport Union (RMT).
[2 marks – accurate with exemplification]

People may join a trade union to protect their rights at work. For example, rail workers join the Rail, Maritime and Transport Union (RMT). The trade union will take action on their behalf eg the RMT met with Transport for London ahead of planned industrial action to try to negotiate a deal on behalf of their members and avoid further industrial action taking place.
[4 marks – accurate point with development and detailed exemplification]

Credit reference to aspects of the following:

Trade Unions
- Protect rights at work eg health and safety, pay, holidays, pensions
- TUs have experience negotiating with management
- TUs have legal teams you can use
- Collective action is more effective than individual action.

Pressure Groups

People may choose to join a pressure group because they are passionate about a cause.
[1 mark – accurate but undeveloped point]

People may choose to join a pressure group because they are passionate about a cause. They may choose to join Greenpeace if they are concerned about the environment.
[2 marks – developed point]

People may choose to join a pressure group because they are passionate about a cause. They may choose to join Greenpeace if they are concerned about the environment. They feel that by joining a pressure group they can have more of an impact by campaigning with other people. For example, Greenpeace has 130,000 UK supporters; this gives it strength in numbers and increases its chances of influencing the government.
[4 marks – accurate point with developed exemplification and analysis]

Credit reference to aspects of the following:

Pressure Groups
- Believe strongly about an issue such as human rights
- Collective action more effective than individual
- Media pay more attention to organised pressure groups
- Pressure groups have experience of campaigning/ protesting
- Seen as the best way to influence government in between elections.

Any valid point that meets the criteria described in the general marking instructions.

7. *Candidates can be credited in a number of ways up to a maximum of 10 marks.*

Possible approaches to answering the question:

Evidence to support Morag's view that the House of Lords does need further reform includes:

Source 2 highlights that less than 5% of the House of Lords has an ethnic-minority background.
[1 mark – accurate use of source 2 but minimal development]

Source 2 highlights that less than 5% of the House of Lords has an ethnic-minority background, which is an under representation, as ethnic minorities make up 13% of the UK population.
[2 marks – accurate use of source 2 with analysis]

Source 2 highlights that the percentage of House of Lords under 60 has decreased from 22% to 16% yet almost three-quarters of the population (77%) are under 60, highlighting under representation of under 60s. This is backed up by source 3 that shows that two peers are under the age of 40 but more than ten times that number are over the age of 90.
[3 marks – accurate information from two sources with analysis]

Credit reference to aspects of the following:
- None of the 790 members are directly elected (source 1)
- Women and disabled are also under represented (source 2)
- The number of privately educated lords is 50% which is disproportionate to the UK population of 7% (source 2)
- Lord Tyler states that House of Lords was "London's best day centre for the elderly" with members able to claim up to £300 per day in expenses for just "turning up and shuffling off"

Evidence to oppose Morag's view that the House of Lords does not need further reform includes:

Source 1 highlights that many Lords bring great experience and expertise to Parliament.
[1 mark – accurate use of source 1 but minimal development]

Source 1 highlights that many Lords bring great experience and expertise to Parliament in the field of medicine, law, business and science and this is supported by source 3 which states that the House of Lords can be useful when opposing bills in the House of Parliament.
[2 marks – accurate use of two sources]

Source 1 highlights that many Lords bring great experience and expertise to Parliament in the field of medicine, law, business and science and this is supported by source 3 which states that the House of Lords can be useful when opposing bills in the House of Parliament. Source 3 also highlights that House of Lords can play a valuable role in scrutinising and revising legislation.
[3 marks – well developed point; accurate use of two sources]

Credit reference to aspects of the following:
- In 1995 there were 7% women in the Lords, in 2015 about 25% were women (source 2)
- Two of the Lord Speakers have been female – Baroness D'Souza & Baroness Hayman (source 1)
- Lack of enthusiasm for change from both houses as well as the British public (source 3)
- Disabled members have increased by 9% (source 2)

- In 1995 over half of the members were hereditary peers whereas today approximately 90% of members are life peers (source 1).

Any valid point that meets the criteria described in the general marking instruction.

Part C: Social Inequality

8. *Candidates can be credited in a number of ways **up to a maximum of 4 marks**.*

Possible approaches to answering the question:

The Government has tried to reduce the inequalities experienced by women/ethnic minorities/elderly by passing laws.

[1 mark – accurate but undeveloped point]

The Government has tried to reduce the inequalities faced by women by passing the Equality Act which makes it illegal to pay women less if they are doing the same job as men.

[2 marks – accurate point with development]

The Government has tried to reduce the inequalities faced by the disabled by passing laws such as the Equality Act in 2010 which makes it illegal to discriminate against a disabled person in the areas of employment and education. In the area of employment, employers cannot treat disabled people differently and must provide disabled employees with special equipment to help them do their job.

[3 marks – accurate, well developed point with exemplification]

Credit reference to aspects of the following:
- Sex Discrimination Act (Women)
- Women on Board Report (Women)
- Race Relations Act (Ethnic Minorities)
- Inclusive Communication
- Disabled people are also protected by the UN Convention on the Rights of Persons with Disabilities (CRPD)
- Office for Disability Issues
- The Equalities & Human Rights Commission
- Equality Advisory & Support Service (EASS)
- Making Sport Inclusive Programme
- Forced Marriage (Civil Protection) Act 2007 – Forced Marriage Protection Order (FMPO)
- Government Campaigns: One Scotland, Show Racism the Red Card etc.

Any other valid point that meets the criteria described in the general marking instruction.

9. *Candidates can be credited in a number of ways **up to a maximum of 6 marks**.*

Possible approaches to answering the question:

Some people have a better standard of living because they have a good job.

[1 mark – accurate but undeveloped point]

Some people have a better standard of living because they have a good job that pays well, such as a teacher.

[2 marks – accurate point with exemplification]

Some people have a better standard of living because they have a good job that pays well, such as a teacher. This may be because they have a number of qualifications, such as a degree, having gone to university for several years.

[3 marks – accurate point with development and exemplification]

Some people are economically disadvantaged because of their family structure. Single parents, for example, may find it harder to find a well-paid job. A two parent family is likely to have a much higher income. Even if a lone parent has good qualifications they can only work at certain times as their child care costs are too high. A family with two parents has a better standard of living; as a result, this may have a positive impact on the education and health of their children.

[4 marks – relevant, accurate point with development, analysis and exemplification]

Credit reference to aspects of the following:
- Employment
- Skills and experience
- Number of dependent children
- Education/training
- Poor health: unable to work due to illness
- Racial discrimination
- Gender discrimination
- Criminal record makes it difficult to find work
- Access to healthcare
- Housing/environment
- Inheritance.

Any other valid point that meets the criteria described in the general marking instructions.

10. *Candidates can be credited in a number of ways **up to a maximum of 6 marks**.*

Possible approaches to answering the question:

Ethnic minorities still face inequality in society because they still face racism in some areas of society.

[1 mark – accurate but undeveloped point]

Older people still face inequality in society because they face discrimination in the world of work because some employers think they don't have IT skills.

[2 marks – accurate with development]

Women still face inequality in society because of sexism. Employers, for example, might not want to employ a woman as they think she will need time off to look after her children. This means that women find it more difficult to find suitable work and as a result often work part-time in occupations like cleaning, childcare etc. Many women feel that the glass ceiling still exists which limits opportunities for promotion in their careers.

[4 marks – accurate point with development, analysis and exemplification]

Credit reference to aspects of the following:
- Ethnic minorities: prejudice, language barriers, poor educational attainment, higher unemployment rates, specific health issues
- Older people: ageism; financial preparation for retirement; previous occupation; family support; changes to benefit system, ie bedroom tax and employability
- Women: sexism; glass ceiling; pay gap; employment in 5Cs, child care availability and costs
- Disabled: prejudice; over qualification; lack of work experience; family support network; continuing health issues; reliance on benefits
- Lone parents: prejudice, family commitments, lack of qualifications, no support network/child care
- Unemployed: stigma of long term unemployment, lack of experience
- Changes to the benefit system/recession.

Any other valid point that meets the criteria described in the general marking instructions.

Part D: Crime and the Law

11. *Candidates can be credited in a number of ways* **up to a maximum of 4 marks.**

    Possible approaches to answering the question:

    The Scottish Government has tried to tackle crime by lowering drink-drive limits.
    [1 mark – accurate but undeveloped point]

    The Scottish Government has tried to tackle crime by making drink-drive limits clearer by reducing the maximum limit; this means that there should be fewer road traffic accidents, deaths and injuries.
    [2 marks – accurate point with development]

    The Scottish Government has tried to tackle crime by making drink-drive limits clearer by reducing the maximum limit; this means that there should be fewer road traffic accidents, deaths and injuries. People are less likely now to drink at all if driving given that the legal limit has been lowered from 80 mg to 50 mg of alcohol in every 100 ml of blood.
    [3 marks – accurate point with development and exemplification]

    Credit reference to aspects of the following:
    - Early release from prison
    - Operation Blade
    - Anti-sectarian legislation
    - Neighbourhood watch
    - CCTV
    - Speed cameras
    - Tags/alternatives to prison
    - ASBOs
    - Supervision orders/tagging orders
    - Community policing.

    Any other valid point that meets the criteria described in the general marking instructions.

12. *Candidates can be credited in a number of ways* **up to a maximum of 6 marks.**

    Possible approaches to answering the question:

    Some people are more affected by crime if they are the victim of a crime.
    [1 mark – accurate but undeveloped point]

    Some people are more affected by crime if they are the victim of a crime. Victims of assault may be fearful that it could happen and may be afraid to leave their home.
    [2 marks – accurate point with development]

    Some people are more affected by crime if they are the victim of a crime. Victims of assault may be fearful that it could happen and may be afraid to leave their home. They may also have alarm systems fitted in their home, at a cost, in order to try to feel more secure.
    [3 marks – accurate point with development and exemplification]

    Credit reference to aspects of the following:
    - Businesses – insurance premiums may rise in areas with high crime rate
    - Perpetrators – loss of family, job, house should they be found guilty/given prison sentence
    - Community – closure of businesses/facilities due to crime/vandalism/robbery
    - Families of perpetrators – targeted by others in the community

    - Some people are more vulnerable to crime – ethnic minorities, young people, elderly.

    Any other valid point that meets the criteria described in the general marking instructions.

13. *Candidates can be credited in a number of ways* **up to a maximum of 6 marks.**

    Possible approaches to answering the question:

    Drug addiction can cause crime.
    [1 mark – accurate but undeveloped point]

    Drug addiction can cause crime. Drug addicts need to pay for their drugs and may steal to fund their habit.
    [2 marks – accurate point with development]

    Drug addiction can cause crime. Drug addicts need to pay for their drugs and may to steal to fund their habit and are more likely to be arrested for crimes such as burglary, shoplifting, robbery or handling stolen goods. Areas with high rates of drug problems are more likely to have high levels of crime.
    [3 marks – accurate point with development and exemplification]

    Credit reference to aspects of the following:
    - Poverty/deprivation
    - Peer pressure
    - Family influence
    - Alcohol abuse
    - Mental illness
    - Violent media images
    - Homelessness
    - Poor educational attainment
    - Social exclusion
    - Greed – white collar crime.

    Any other valid point that meets the criteria described in the general marking instructions.

14. *Candidates can be credited in a number of ways* **up to a maximum of 10 marks.**

    Possible approaches to answering the question:

    Option 1: Ban Legal Highs

    The Government should ban legal highs as legal highs have been linked to hospital admissions for things such as poisoning, mental health issues, and in extreme cases death.
    [1 mark – evidence drawn from source 1]

    The Government should ban legal highs as legal highs have been linked to hospital admissions for things such as poisoning, mental health issues, and in extreme cases death. This is backed up in source 2 which shows that there has been an increase in deaths as a result of legal highs.
    [2 marks – evidence linked from Source 1 and Source 2]

    The Government should ban legal highs as legal highs have been linked to hospital admissions for things such as poisoning, mental health issues, and in extreme cases death. This is backed up in source 2 which shows that there has been an increase in deaths as a result of legal highs. The increase in deaths has gone from just over 40 to almost 120, which is almost triple the number.
    [3 marks – evidence linked from source 1 and Source 2 with evaluative comment]

    Credit reference to aspects of the following:
    - These drugs are often included in everyday household products and are often labelled not for human consumption (source 1).

- Mandeep Khan states that "more of my time as a paramedic is being taken up dealing with the consequences of legal highs. The misuse of these drugs diverts our attention from cases that are much more important" (source 3).

Reasons for rejecting the other option:

I rejected Option 2 as although source 2 states 66% of young people know that legal highs could result in death source 1 highlights that the UK has the most severe problem with legal highs in Western Europe, with significant numbers of young people regularly admitting to taking legal highs.

[2 marks – evidence linked from source 1 and source 2]

Option 2: Do not ban Legal Highs

The Government should not ban legal highs as there was a mass demonstration against the proposed legislation due to the inclusion of nitrous oxide, otherwise known as laughing gas, within the bill. Nitrous oxide is commonly used as anaesthetic during dentistry, childbirth and as a mood enhancer.

[1 mark – evidence drawn from source 1]

The Government should not ban legal highs as in a recent survey 53% of 16–25 year olds stated that they had never taken legal highs with a further 10% only ever having taken them once (source 2). This is supported by source 1 when it states that despite media attention around half of young people have never experimented with legal highs.

[2 marks – evidence linked from source 1 and source 2]

Credit reference to aspects of the following:
- Control and monitoring of legal highs is very difficult (source 3)
- Often new versions are created and sold just as fast as the Government can ban them (source 3)
- There has been little or no research into the long term or short term risks of taking legal highs (source 1).

Reasons for rejecting the other option:

I rejected Option 1 as although Mandeep Khan states that lots of people are unaware of the dangers of legal highs source 2 highlights that 66% of young people know that legal highs result in death.

[2 marks – evidence linked from source 2 and source 3]

Any other valid reason that meets the criteria described in the general marking instructions.

Part E: World Powers

15. *Candidates can be credited in a number of ways **up to a maximum of 4 marks.***

Possible approaches to answering the question:

USA

In America, Barack Obama introduced a new health care law, nicknamed Obamacare.

[1 mark – accurate point]

In America, Barack Obama introduced a new health care law called the Affordable Care Act (Obamacare). The Act was designed to increase the affordability and quality of health insurance and lower the number of uninsured. This has helped many people, especially those on low incomes, younger people and ethnic minorities.

[3 marks – accurate point with development and exemplification]

Credit reference to aspects of the following:
- Medicare, Medicaid and State Children's Health Insurance Program (covers children who do not qualify for Medicaid)
- Temporary Assistance for Needy Families (TANF)
- Affirmative Action programmes as they apply today eg the Supreme Court has basically ruled that consideration of an applicant's race/ethnicity is legal
- American Recovery and Reinvestment Act 2009 - provides expansion of unemployment benefits, social welfare provision, education and health care
- No Child Left Behind (NCLB) 2001 – aimed to improve performance in public schools to improve qualifications/employability of all children. Backed with big increases in federal funding but on-going debate as to success
- Race to the Top is a $4.35 billion United States Department of Education contest created to spur innovation and reforms in state and local district education. It is funded as part of the American Recovery and Reinvestment Act of 2009
- Funded as part of the American Recovery and Reinvestment Act of 2009
- Food stamps now known as Supplemental Nutrition Assistance Programme (SNAP) to provide healthy food for poor families
- Federal minimum wage.

China

Today most farms operate as private businesses and decisions about what to produce and how to produce are made by farmers. The government created the Household Responsibility System. Farmers have to give a certain amount to the government, but any surplus is kept by the farmer. This means that poor farmers are allowed to sell their goods for a profit thus reducing inequality.

[3 marks – accurate point with development and exemplification]

Credit reference to aspects of the following:
- Dismantling of work permit system (Hukou)
- Foreign investment, encouragement of private business (Open Door Policy and Special Economic Zones)
- Encouraging rural areas and small towns to develop entrepreneurs and industrial growth (Township and Village Enterprises)
- Development of social security system
- Better rights for women
- Improving health services, housing and reducing crime.

South Africa

Credit reference to aspects of the following:
- Affirmative Action
- Black Economic Empowerment (BEE)
- Programmes to ensure everyone has access to drinkable water, sanitation and electricity
- Land redistribution policy.

Any other valid point that meets the criteria described in the general marking instruction.

16. *Candidates can be credited in a number of ways **up to a maximum of 6 marks.***

Possible approaches to answering the question:

Citizens in the US have the right to vote for a candidate in an election.

[1 mark – accurate point]

Citizens in the US have the right to vote for a candidate in an election. In 2016, millions of people voted for Hilary Clinton in the Presidential Election.

[2 marks – accurate point with exemplification]

People in China have the right to vote in village elections. This allows citizens the opportunity to elect village committees and village leaders as a form of local democracy. The elected representatives are entrusted with managing local affairs.

[3 marks – accurate, well developed point]

Credit reference to aspects of the following:

Clear reference to specific aspects of political systems of chosen G20 country.
- Standing for election
- Voting in elections at various levels
- Participating in political parties, trade unions, pressure groups
- Free speech
- Freedom of press
- Protection by the law.

Any other valid point that meets the criteria described in the general marking instructions.

17. *Candidates can be credited in a number of ways up to a maximum of 6 marks.*

Possible approaches to answering the question:

The USA has the ability to influence other countries due to the size of its military.

[1 mark – undeveloped point]

The USA has the ability to influence other countries due to the size of its military. The USA military is often referred to as the 'world policeman' and has been able to influence countries such as Afghanistan and Libya.

[2 marks – accurate point with development]

Brazil has the ability to influence other countries due to the fact it is a growing economy and is a member of BRICS. Brazil is also the single biggest supplier of agricultural products to the European Union so is a crucial trading partner. Furthermore Brazil has recently been influential in the 'South-South' Cooperation, becoming a donor to developing African countries, providing $23 million dollars to Mozambique to help with the development of HIV/AIDs treatments. This cooperation is seen as being more influential than the 'tied aid' models of the past.

[4 marks – well explained point, with exemplification and analysis]

Credit reference to aspects of the following:
- Trade
- Defence
- Diplomatic support
- Ideology
- Immigration
- Culture.

Any other valid point that meets the criteria described in the general marking instructions.

18. *Candidates can be credited in a number of ways up to a maximum of 4 marks.*

Possible approaches to answering the question:

African Union has deployed peacekeepers in Burundi.

[1 mark – accurate point]

NATO has continued to try to bring stability in Iraq. They have recently introduced military medicine courses to train new paramedics and have provided support with the maintenance of tanks and armoured vehicles.

[2 marks – accurate point with exemplification]

Oxfam attempts to address famine in South Sudan. In 2016 Oxfam helped more than 600,000 people across the country by providing food and water. Oxfam helped to build and repair boreholes and wells, test quality levels, treat water, and train people to look after and maintain their own water supply.

[3 marks – developed point with detailed exemplification]

Credit reference to aspects of the following:
- UNICEF
- WHO
- UNESCO
- FAO
- AU ceasefire monitors in Darfur
- AU force in Somalia
- Oxfam – supporting refugees in Syria with clean drinking water, relief supplies, improving sanitation and giving information on rights
- Oxfam – Malawi food crisis – reached over 400,000 people with assistance, including cash to buy food, tools to improve crops and seeds including more resilient options to drought such as sweet potato vines.

Any other valid point that meets the criteria described in the general marking instructions.

19. *Candidates can be credited in a number of ways up to a maximum of 6 marks.*

Possible approaches to answering the question:

Issue – Underdevelopment in Africa

Many people in African countries do not have access to appropriate levels of healthcare.

[1 mark – accurate but undeveloped point]

Many people in African countries do not have access to appropriate levels of healthcare and as a result many people die each year from illnesses such as malaria.

[2 marks – accurate point with development]

Some poorer African countries have inadequate healthcare with too few doctors and nurses. This makes it more difficult to treat preventable illnesses such as diarrhoeal diseases. Each day over 2000 children die from diarrhoeal diseases around the world, more than AIDS, malaria and measles.

[3 marks – accurate point with development and exemplification]

Credit reference to aspects of the following:
- Unsafe water/poor sanitary conditions
- Low life expectancy/high infant mortality rates
- High illiteracy rates/low levels of education (including attendance)
- Gender inequalities
- Refugees
- Piracy
- Child soldiers
- Destroyed infrastructure
- Human rights abuses
- Effects of terrorism
- Restrictions to civil liberties.

Any other valid point that meets the criteria described in the general marking instruction.

20. *Candidates can be credited in a number of ways up to a maximum of 6 marks.*

Possible approaches to answering the question:

Some international organisations are unsuccessful at tackling international terrorism because they do not get enough help from member countries.
[1 mark – accurate but undeveloped point]

NATO's methods are unsuccessful at tackling international terrorism because although it is a very powerful military alliance, terrorists are often not easily identifiable. They are not like a country which would be easier for NATO to fight against in the traditional sense. Terrorists don't wear uniforms and don't stick to one country's borders.
[3 marks – accurate developed point with exemplification]

NATO can't support people who have come under threat from their own governments. Since 2011 it has not been able to stop the ongoing conflict between the two warring factions in Libya and as a result it has been unable to protect civilians effectively. NATO is not set up to help install new governments and ensure security and stability in places like Libya; it was only effective in the military conflict against Colonel Gaddafi. After this, NATO members did not want the expense of rebuilding the country in the long term.
[4 marks – accurate developed point with exemplification and analysis]

Credit reference to aspects of the following:
• Lack of training of local security services
• Tribal/Civil War in Africa
• Corrupt government
• Sanctions affect some countries more than others
• The extent of poverty
• Financial constraints
• Lack of cooperation
• Inappropriate aid
• Unfair trade
• Fair trade
• Increased access to anti-retroviral therapy
• Increased enrolment in education
• Success of UN Specialised Agencies
• Success of Sustainable Development Goals.

Any other valid point that meets the criteria described in the general marking instructions.

21. *Candidates can be credited in a number of ways up to a maximum of 10 marks.*

Possible approaches to answering the question:

The problem of crime in Japan compared to other countries

Conclusion: Compared to many other countries there are relatively low levels of crime in Japan.
[1 mark for a valid conclusion]

Conclusion: Compared to many other countries there are relatively low levels of crime in Japan.

Evidence: Japan had 22 crimes per 1000 people in 2014 (source 1), which is only about one quarter of the EU figure of 80 and lower than all the countries mentioned (source 2).
[3 marks – valid conclusion with evidence from two sources and evaluative terminology]

The effects of the changing population structure in Japan

Conclusion: As the elderly population increases so do social and economic problems in Japan.
[1 mark for a valid conclusion]

Conclusion: As the elderly population increases so do social and economic problems in Japan.

Evidence: Source 1 highlights that increased poverty and a different population structure will make old age pensions and elderly care very expensive in the future. As source 2 shows the elderly population will almost double in 40 years but those paying tax (15–64 years) will fall to just over 50% of the population.
[3 marks for a valid conclusion with supporting evidence and evaluative terminology]

Also credit reference to:
• Housing is getting expensive as a result of the aging population (source 3); 61% own their home, lower than the EU, France, Italy and Argentina
• Japan has a high life expectancy (source 3) but this will be difficult to maintain as fewer will be paying tax (source 3)
• A growing elderly population is listed as one of Japan's problems (source 1).

The effect of poverty on working age women

Conclusion: Poverty decreases the happiness level of working age women.
[1 mark for a valid conclusion]

Conclusion: Poverty decreases the happiness level of working age women.

Evidence: Source 1 highlights that one third of working age women now live in poverty with part time work preventing women from having financial savings; this is a massive worry for Japanese women. This is supported by source 3 which highlights that the average happiness level for women is 4.67 (out of 10) but for working age women it is only 3.2 which is almost half of the average happiness level for men.
[3 marks for valid conclusion with supporting evidence and evaluation]

The country most like Japan

Conclusion: South Korea is most like Japan.
[1 mark for a valid conclusion]

Conclusion: South Korea is most like Japan.

Evidence: In South Korea the poverty rate is 16.5% and in Japan it is 16% (sources 1 and 2).
[2 marks for a valid conclusion with supporting evidence]

Conclusion: South Korea is most like Japan.

Evidence: In South Korea only 0·5% more people in poverty; this is the closest to Japan at 16% with crime rate in South Korea also being closest to that of Japan – 22 per 1000 in Japan and 32 per 1000 in South Korea.
[3 marks for valid conclusion with supporting evidence and evaluation]

Also credit reference to:
• Internet users – 865 per 1000 in Japan and South Korea – highest of all the countries mentioned (sources 1 and 3).

Any other valid point that meets the criteria described in the general marking instructions.

Acknowledgements

Permission has been sought from all relevant copyright holders and Hodder Gibson is grateful for the use of the following:

Image © Point Fr/Shutterstock.com (2015 page 4);
Image © Goodluz/Shutterstock.com (2015 page 4);
Image © Blend Images/Shutterstock.com (2015 page 8);
Image © Dean Drobot/Shutterstock.com (2015 page 8);
Image © Mahesh Patil/Shutterstock.com (2015 pages 20 & 24);
An extract adapted from the article 'Organised gangs using technology to evade police' taken from BBC News, 29 December 2015 (www.bbc.co.uk/news/uk-scotland-35190233) © BBC (2017 page 17);
'Better Life Index Study' adapted from www.oecdbetterlifeindex.org © OECD Publishing, Paris (2017 SQP page 15).